ADVANCE PRAISE FOR
YOUR LIFE, YOUR WAY

Alicia Lamberghini-West's book, *Your Life, Your Way: Become Aware of Social Pressures Limiting Women*, is the ideal guide for every woman in our culture, no matter how liberated she may already be, or however hopeless her situation might feel. Drawing on her many years of experience as a clinical psychologist, and aware of every trap our culture sets for women, Lamberghini-West helps us understand what might be holding us back, and then, in clear, simple terms, what to do about it. *Indeed, she is the therapist every woman wishes she'd had,* and I'll be drawing on her wisdom and recommending *Your Life, Your Way* for years to come.
— Rosemary Daniell, author of *Secrets of the Zona Rosa: How Writing (and Sisterhood) Can Change Women's Lives*, and eight other books of poetry and prose

This book addresses a major challenge for women: how do you reach into your own psyche and identify the gender assumptions and rules instilled in you since birth? After you accomplish that, you can begin to consider whether you now agree with those assumptions and rules. If you decide you don't accept them, you have to consider the consequences of changing and decide what you're going to do. *It won't be easy, but it might be worthwhile.*
— Nada L Stotland, MD, MPH, Professor of Psychiatry, Rush University, Chicago

TO DR. AQUINO,
    WITH GRATITUDE !

Alicia Lamberghini-West, PsyD

Alicia West

10/27/2021

YOUR
LIFE,
YOUR
WAY

Become Aware of Social
Pressures Limiting Women

Printed and bound in the United States of America
ISBN: 978-0-578-40100-3
Library of Congress Control Number: 2018914755

DEDICATION

To my husband Greg, our daughter Pilar,
and our grandson Marco,
with special gratitude for their unconditional presence.

TABLE OF CONTENTS

PREFACE

Somebody said that psychologists never retire: first they practice, then they teach, and finally, they write. I have been a clinical psychologist since 1985 and enjoyed the first two stages of my career, but I find I appreciate this third stage of writing the most. Creating this book has brought change into my life, and I am happy about that.

I have had a lifelong, profound interest in the topic of this book: *the social pressures and related challenges that women of all ages and sociocultural backgrounds face, and how they can deal with them.*

Nine of my twenty-five years in private practice as a psychologist were particularly significant. During that period, I worked in an outpatient program with an all-female staff and client base. All the doctors, staff, and patients were women. I come from a family in which, except for my mother and me, everyone is male. Being surrounded by all-female energy was a new and positive experience for me.

At this clinic, I learned two things that have stayed with me since: the first is how many social pressures women face and how unhappy, guilty, or ashamed we feel if we do not rise to meet them. I saw this firsthand, not only among clients but also in my own life and in my interactions with the other doctors and staff. The second thing I learned is that when a woman helps another woman, most of the time the woman helping is reliable, committed, and efficient. When a woman supports another woman, both succeed.

This time in my career helped me formulate the objective of this book: helping my readers *identify and manage the pressures they feel from family, com-*

munity, and society because of their expectations, and the pressures women place on themselves based on internalizing those expectations. In general, cultural or social stereotypes generate expectations, expectations create demands, and demands are the source of pressures.[1]

The reason I wrote this book is to show women that, while our particular cultural and social environments influence us, we have *a personal identity that is unique*, and we have the right to develop, expand, and express it. The more we grow, the more happiness we will have in life.

Besides, social pressures and expectations are not laws, and not conforming to them does not make us bad people. We have the freedom to accept, reject, or negotiate these social pressures according to our thoughts, experiences, and preferences.

The starting point for a woman's evaluation of her circumstances, goals, needs, and wishes is the fact that *her life is her own*. Women are not objects or the property of others. Our lives are our own, and this gives us power.

I wrote this book with the following people in mind:

- Women who are interested in these topics and would like to expand their knowledge
- Women who feel restricted in their life and decision-making
- Women who are trapped in guilt and shame for not responding in expected ways
- Women who are in the middle of stress, strain, and tension provoked by the conflict between personal and social expectations
- Women who experience negative consequences related to the previous points and suffer physical, psychological, and interpersonal problems
- Women who want to grow and increase resilience, self-esteem, and self-worth concerning their identity
- Men who want to help women in this journey

I started putting my observations together, first to learn and understand on a personal level, then to help my clients in private practice and education, and now, through writing this book, to reach many more women. This is important to me because it is through women that the world is changing, we play a crucial role in the development of new generations and in maintaining forward progress.

This book is also for men because *undoing social pressures is everyone's responsibility*. It is only from a foundation of freedom and equitable distribution of power between men and women that a new and better world can develop—with each willing to give, take, and share their life with each other.

Here is my message to my sisters around the world: Keep reaching beyond what feels easy, secure, and cozy in your life. Try new experiences. Allow yourself to make mistakes and learn from them. *From change, courage, and creativity, a more inspired, resourceful, and powerful identity will emerge to serve you and others in pursuing a wholehearted life and being the best you can be.*

Sharing this message is my personal mission and a way of giving back for the opportunities and the good I have received in my life, for which I am so grateful.

INTRODUCTION

My whole life I have been observing and learning about women, starting with my grandmother, who was passive, patient, and resigned; then my mother, a woman who lived during a time of transition, and was both submissive and resistant. I grew up with three brothers and had no definite place other than on my own. I spent much time trying to understand what I wanted and wondering how much freedom of choice I could have in life. As I grew older, I continued listening and learning through daily life, going through my stages, traveling, studying, and eventually becoming a psychologist.

I saw women trying to be perfect, inside and out, and feeling miserable when they could not look or act as they imagined they should. I saw women blaming themselves when a challenge got the better of them. Instead of considering how hard the problem was or treating their limits with respect, they thought they were in the wrong for not trying harder or doing better.

I saw women search for validation amid our society's impossible-to-achieve beauty standards, only to experience suffering and frustration. I watched them attempt strict, nonstop diets and workout regimens or surgery to correct, reduce, enlarge, or otherwise change their body, rather than accepting and appreciating their unique appearance, treating their body—their person—with consideration and love.

I saw women take a checklist approach to life: there were "to-dos" they felt obligated to check off, like getting married and having children, even when these were not their personal goals or they were not ready to make these significant life changes. I saw women ashamed of being single in a world that does not understand why a woman might choose to be on her own. I saw women distressed by trying to explain their decision not to have children while other women judged and tried to dissuade them.

I saw highly competent women take second-place roles because they believed this was the correct "place" for women. I saw women exhaust their resources to gain others' approval and be seen as a "good woman," even though they were overextended in their responsibilities, undervalued, and sometimes even abused.

I saw women in difficult marriages, with unfaithful and abusive husbands, who never considered the possibility of separation or divorce. I saw many women assume that the failures in their relationship were because of them. I listened to women blame themselves for being unable to change their partner or take responsibility for his problems. I saw women lie for men, lie to men, justify men, forgive men. I saw women hide their relationship difficulties because of shame or guilt and blame themselves for what had happened with their partner or husband.

I saw women try to "have it all" and show everyone their perfect, balanced, lucky life. They worried that if they were missing even one component in life, people would say something was wrong with them.

I saw women try to get into or maintain a career even though they had other priorities. They felt the times no longer allowed them to prioritize raising their children or to follow a different life path.

I saw women remain silent when sexually harassed, scared of losing their job, reputation, and future opportunities—often blaming themselves and suffering embarrassment, shame, and anxiety for something for which they were not responsible.

I saw insecure women who had no power outside their home and so imposed dictatorial reign over their household, trying to manage their husband and children; struggling to look perfect; gossiping and putting other women down to increase their significance; talking loudly to be sure they were heard; reacting with anger to the slightest inconvenience. All because they were unsure of themselves, needed their value to be affirmed, and needed to feel they had some control.

I saw women trade their potential or independence for the comfort and security their partner provided. The more they received from him, the more obligated they were to comply with his wishes, to smile and look beautiful. From the outside, these women seemed happy, privileged, and flourishing. However, in the privacy of personal conversations, I saw them cry or, alternatively, deny their husband's indiscretions, explain away his actions, or blame themselves for what was happening. I saw women ashamed or guilty for what men did to them, convinced the abuse or mistreatment was "fair" because they did not perform according to expectations.

I also saw women with a healthy respect for themselves as individuals, who planned their lives based on conscious recognition of their wishes, who grew through constructive relationships with themselves and others. These women also faced social pressures, but they managed them productively. They cultivated enthusiastic discipline and drive toward the objectives that made life meaningful to them.

Though on the whole, I saw a few instances of women being loved and treated well. Moreover, it was difficult to acknowledge that I did not see many examples of good, fulfilling relationships and interactions between men and women.

What sustains these difficult scenarios women face are the *pressures that society, including families and communities, put on women*. From the idea that there is a definite way things are and should be done, to messaging from parents and family members that it is a virtue to always put everyone but yourself first, to traditional and religious principles that maintain that a woman's spot is second place, and that following traditions and customs makes a woman "good" and worthy.

These social pressures on women have roots in *patriarchal principles and traditions*. Men are given predominance over women; expectations are generated—including that men are providers and women are caretakers—and women are relegated to second-tier status, explicitly or implicitly. The power is on the side of the provider, who has authority to dictate what happens in the relationship. On the other hand, the woman should please the man and follow his directions. This setup of predetermined expectations and responses becomes *a controlling factor in the external and internal lives of women*.

Women also face pressure as they try to implement *feminist principles*, which highlight a woman's right to freedom, independence, and equal opportunity. Here the emphasis is often on women making themselves the focal point of their decisions, plus developing their skills and potential as the most critical endeavor of life.

The reality is that we women often *feel caught between the expectations coming at us from the two directions of patriarchal ideology and feminism*— the demands of our social reality and the pressures of living up to the goals we set for ourselves. As a result, we experience a lot of conflict over which set of expectations to respond to. We feel uncertain about following a path that society says is a "woman's destiny," or that centers on fulfilling our parents and communities' expectations. One the other end, we may think we are not good enough, or we try to fix or hide what we perceive to be our shortcomings and failures.

In this struggle to fit in with one side or the other, or both, *we lose touch with our authentic self.* We focus on trying to respond to social expectations instead of attending to our inner life and what makes us who we genuinely are. All the while, we search for meaning in our lives, a sense of control, and validation of our deepest self.

To be part of the solution, you first have to understand the problem, its nature, dimension, and severity—and specifically, how the issue might affect you as an individual. In the first part of this book, I identify the central social pressures that pose limitations on women's freedom and offer advice for dealing with these forces. In the second part, I talk about real-life situational or personal contexts women might experience. And in part three, I discuss how social pressures and power dynamics often combine to affect women's lives.

I focus on the importance of developing a *healthy sense of self*—a strong personal identity, which is the backbone of our being. I talk about the importance of attitudes and our state of mind in facing new situations or responding to expectations. I touch on *shame and guilt*, how they interact with social pressures, and how you can *increase your resilience* in the face of adversity.

Throughout this book, I use storytelling to illustrate the pressures and issues I am writing about. The stories are connected to the concept presented, to exemplify that idea in a precise moment and specific circumstances. These stories are based on my personal experiences and real-life cases from my practice as a psychologist. I have changed names and combined some elements of these stories, so individuals are not identifiable in any way, but the situations and issues described are nonetheless real.

My main hope is that reading this book will give you a deeper understanding of the social pressures women experience and where they come from. These social customs and traditions are often rooted in patriarchy and sexist thinking passed down from generation to generation.

Each person's identity has two roots: one is cultural, related to our social context; the other is personal, unique to us. We need to find a balance between the two and develop the positive aspects of both to have a healthy identity. However, many of us have given more space to the sociocultural piece of our identity, so we are out of balance. I want to help women *gain freedom from the sociocultural self and strengthen the personal self.*

I also want to encourage you to use this information to look at your own life. If any of these pressures are weighing you down and causing limitations, know that you do not have to live your life that way. You have the freedom to cultivate your identity and grow your destiny in the way that is best for you. You can say yes to your desires and goals. You can choose on your terms. You can live *your life your way.*

We can change the balance in our identity by first listening to, and respecting, our unique story and appreciating our distinctive characteristics. We can also stop giving so much attention to the cultural self, which is shaped significantly by stereotypes and promotes living up to unrealistic expectations—the source of the pressures we face.

When you finish this book, you will have a greater awareness of the importance of giving yourself more freedom and opportunities to act and to grow as an individual. This can lead to a greater appreciation of the amazing person you are and recognition of the importance of pursuing a fulfilling life.

I wrote this book thinking about women who are exposed to strong cultural pressures that limit their expectations, and women who are unhappy with the expectations others have set for them. However, this book is dedicated to women of all backgrounds, social classes, ages, and cultures, both traditional and nontraditional. It can also be useful for parents, partners, teachers, mentors, advisors, counselors, psychologists, and psychiatrists who want to support women in the fundamental task of developing a healthy personal identity.

Creating this book has been a meaningful process for me, with material drawn from my experiences, thoughts, and lessons learned over many years. However, this process is incomplete without you, the reader. So *I thank you for joining me on this journey to greater freedom and joy.*

PART 1

THE SOCIAL PRESSURES
WOMEN FACE

1

Social Pressures on Women [1]

As you know, being a woman is not easy. Women around the world face significant challenges, because women of all cultural backgrounds, ages, and socioeconomic status are exposed to cultural stereotypes and expectations that outline how they "should be" physically and psychologically, the "right" feelings and emotions they should have and express, what thoughts are "proper," and how they should plan their lives.

In many cases, we try to comply with the expectations of our culture and society, even when it means putting aside our hopes and dreams. Why do the pressures and requirements that come with social expectations weigh us down? Why do we experience barriers to striving for our ideas, goals, and wishes? *What is in the way of pursuing our desires and potential?*

Stereotypes create an idealized image, a type of blueprint for us to follow, and if we conform to these ideals, we are "real" and "good" women. Society evaluates a woman positively if she follows the standards laid out for her. However, if she does not comply with society's expectations, she is evaluated negatively—there is something "wrong" with her. This results in worry, feelings of insecurity, and vulnerability to feelings of shame or guilt. It affects not only the woman but also her intimate circle.[1] I have seen many women put up with these pressures in an attempt to be respected and accepted into various social groups, even when doing so puts their own identity and growth at risk.

Cultural stereotypes and gender stereotypes of the "best" way to be and do things generate expectations in the people who play a pivotal role in our upbringing: parents, relatives, teachers, community leaders, and the like. Soon, these expectations become *the norm* and are thought of as "natural"—just the way men and women are, the way they behave, the way they think, the roles they "naturally" play.[1]

It is essential to consider the following two points: First, gender stereotypes are rooted in traditional patriarchal ideology, which establishes specific and opposite roles for men and women and power differences between genders, with the masculine role having the control and the feminine role being powerless.[2]

Second, because gender stereotypes have been around for so long, they are accepted as "rules," and violating these gender stereotypes leads to negative retribution and reduced worth.[3,4] For this reason, it is difficult to go against the grain of established stereotypes; if we do, we may expose ourselves to hurt and rejection.

Gender stereotypes generate expectations, expectations create demands, and these demands are the source of social pressures. Society has many gender stereotypes that impact expectations for norms and behaviors regarding what is or is not "appropriate" for boys and girls, men and women. Early in life, we learn about these gender stereotypes and related expectations. Because these expectations are taught as an "ideal," it is difficult to consider—or even know it is possible—to confront, deviate from, or ignore them.[1]

The feminine ideal defines what is expected of women, and this ideal is framed in terms of rules for life and living. If a woman meets these expectations, she will be accepted, respected, and rewarded. If she does not reach the expected ideal, she risks negative consequences up to and including abuse.[1]

Just as we are taught what is expected of us, we are also made aware of the likely *risks and consequences of not living up to expectations.* This is one reason women hesitate to take a path other than what is expected and accepted culturally. If a woman takes a less-traveled road, she exposes herself to negative social consequences, self-blame, and judgment.

The negative consequences we self-generate, such as feelings of shame and guilt, happen as a result of *internalizing* society's expectations. We take on our society's cultural ideas about what is "right," as though these are our personal ideas and absolutely true. Consequently, if we went in a different direction than our culture and social groups prescribe, we feel we have done something "wrong" and suffer from shame or guilt.[1]

As you can see, expectations are like tracks and pathways that are easy to stay on because they lead to acceptance, and there are role models to guide us. To choose a different path is difficult, because it may mean diverging in thought or lifestyle from family and close friends and risking their rejection. It is also a potentially lonely choice; we may not have peer support to help us reach our goals or role models to show us it is possible to be different and successful. *Accepting or rejecting expectations plays a significant role in how we develop our lives and perceive our destiny.*

The strength of cultural expectations is *based on the perception that they are "true"* since they come from our family, teachers, and other people we believe love us and want the best for us. In addition, these expectations are relayed to and often imposed on us within the context of an unequal power dynamic, such as parent-child, teacher-student, and leader-follower. There may be little room for the junior member in the relationship to contradict ideas and advice without risking some censure or backlash from the senior member. So expectations are strong because they represent cultural ideals of what is "right" and how things "should be." Compliance will ensure pleasant and enjoyable interactions with society, while noncompliance will lead to the opposite outcome.

For all these reasons, *cultural expectations shape individuals' choices and lifestyles.* This can lead to a type of societal harmony, but it also limits people's life choices and ability to explore their potential. People, in turn, perpetuate the same stereotypes they were exposed to, continuing to strengthen these ideas and influence the behavior of future generations.

Women, in particular, are exposed to all kinds of social pressures that make them feel they have no option other than to be and behave according to the expectations and role models their environment dictates. My message to women is that *it is our right to make our own choices* and to be respected and accepted on the basis of our self-determination rather than because we have followed someone else's expectations. Of course, this is easier said than done. Societal expectations come with attractive-sounding promises of acceptance, belonging, and respect. However, keep in mind that promises and expectations *are two sides of the same coin and grow in proportion to each other.*

Social expectations are relayed in two ways. The first focuses on the "positives," pointing out how meaningful and rewarding life is for women who follow societal expectations. For instance: *"Get a perfect body, and you'll have a perfect life,"* implying that being beautiful is necessary for success and happiness. The second emphasizes the "negatives." For example, if someone does not have a "perfect body," she is perceived as "unattractive," which can devalue her sense of self-worth. This results in feelings of shame and guilt that affect self-esteem and impact personal confidence in current and future endeavors. *Self-esteem is the motor of personal growth.* Someone with high self-esteem may feel there are no limits to what she can do, but when a woman's self-esteem is low, everything seems like an obstacle.

Some women resist the influence of cultural expectations and pressures. They know what they want to do and create, and are willing to go for it, even if it means going outside societal norms and bounds. Sometimes society accepts these women's choices but holds them to an *expectation of perfection.* Brenda's story illustrates this.

Brenda was one of my clients, a woman in her late twenties who had decided to wait on marriage and focus on developing her own business. She faced pressure to have a perfect, outstanding life (wealth, travel options, great social life) and career (success, prestige, networks, growth). Brenda felt that if her choices did not result in exceptional outcomes every time, others would think she had made poor decisions, that something was wrong with her, or that she was a loser. Sometimes she felt this way about herself too. Why? *Because she was doing something other than what was expected for her as a woman, her choices were questioned anytime something did not go perfectly.*

Situations like Brenda's are common today. I describe this scenario as the expectation and pressure on women to make perfect choices the first time around. In other words, if a woman wants to do her own thing or try something new, she has to make sure she does it flawlessly!

WHAT ARE THE CONSEQUENCES OF SOCIAL PRESSURES?

Women are expected to live up to and are evaluated against gender stereotypes of femininity to such a degree that nonconformity causes them worry and concern. These fears are related to the notion that unless a woman does what her family, community, and potential partner expect of her, she will not be accepted and respected. However, by living up to and complying with sociocultural ideals and expectations, she will *find her place in her family and community.*

In traditional cultures, there is an expectation that women will get married. In these environments, there is little room, respect for, or recognition of single women. What happens if a woman in her twenties expresses disinterest in marriage? The consequences could be severe: she may be seen as weird or unhealthy, ostracized and isolated in the community.

On the other side of the coin, since it is expected that a woman will have a husband, a young woman in her twenties follows her parents' advice to get married. She may or may not be attracted to her husband, but this is the least of her concerns. The primary objective of marriage is to secure her place in society and her community's acceptance; maybe later she will fall in love.

With social acceptance comes a sense of *self-respect and self-appreciation*. One of my clients sought treatment because she "didn't want to have kids." When I asked her how she felt about that, she said, "There's *something wrong with me* because I don't have the desire to be a mother."

In a less traditional environment, a woman in the early stages of her career who considers quitting her job to take care of her young children may feel the pressure of social expectations that women should "have it all." She may worry that not continuing her career will make her less of a "modern woman" and *feel embarrassed or guilty about her decision.*

WHAT ARE THE PRESSURES WOMEN FACE?

In both traditional and contemporary cultures, women face intense pressure regarding their *appearance*: to be a certain weight, to be beautiful, and to look youthful. Another common pressure across cultures is the pressure on women *to be perfect*. Women are judged against two possible options: success or *failure*. There is little room for grays or trial and error.

In traditional cultures (conservative, religious, ethnic minority, or rural environments), women are often subjected to the oppression of patriarchal systems and the power differentials this implies. A woman is pressured to follow the expectations of her family of origin. For instance:

- To be dependent, first on her parents and then her husband.
- To get married, preferably at a young age, and to stay married for life. Separation and divorce are not options.
- To have a stable family with children and grandchildren.
- To cultivate domestic skills, such as cooking, cleaning, and child-rearing. She may have some education, but too much or professional training is less desirable. (A highly educated woman can overturn expectations of dominant masculinity and patriarchal norms.)
- To be at the service of her family, putting her needs and wishes after everybody else's. She is responsible for her family's well-being and harmony, which often causes her to overextend herself, to the detriment of her wellness and personal goals.

In contemporary cultures (highly educated, urban, or liberal environments), patriarchal norms still have influence and face off against pressures from feminism, which often results in contradictory messages and expectations for women. In these cultures, the primary pressures are to have it all, be perfect, and achieve balance. For instance:

- To have a successful career, stopping at nothing in pursuit of recognition, prosperity, and power.
- To have a happy, healthy marriage to the perfect man; beautiful, gifted kids; spectacular house; exciting social life; and gorgeous vacations.

- To have an impeccable balance between work and family life, always giving the right amount of focus to the right issue at the right time, so she is always in the moment, energized, and creative. To have a harmonious family life in which each family member hits all the right developmental milestones and social achievements at the proper times with no problems or complaints.
- To maintain her physical appearance—be attractive, thin, and fit—and have holistic harmony in her inner life.

Overall, we can see that universally, across a wide variety of sociocultural contexts, women of all ages and backgrounds consistently face many difficult pressures. Sometimes these pressures combine to create what I call a "pressure cooker" situation. Examples will follow in part one of this book.

Women react to these pressures in different ways. They may try to meet expectations to avoid feelings of shame or guilt for noncompliance, resulting in a life that revolves around pleasing others and meeting their expectations. Alternatively, they may try to build resilience—internal and external resources that determine the development of a person's identity—which is related to growth, and consequently, well-being and health.

It is crucial for women to identify the social pressures that interfere with their life for two reasons: first, *to help themselves have a better life* and, second, *to avoid passing these pressures on to the next generation.*

In this first part of the book, I will present in-depth information and examples of the pressures and issues that women face in different times and contexts, followed by an analysis of the origin of these pressures. I will share my reflections on how women can respond to these pressures with greater self-awareness to increase their freedom and well-being.

2

The Pressure to Be Beautiful, Thin, and Youthful

Carol, a middle-aged woman, told me: "I'm not beautiful, but I have a perfect body, and I'm proud of myself. When I turned 34, I decided to lose weight. I wasn't overweight, but I didn't have a model figure either. I'll never forget how it felt when I finally started losing weight: life was good because I was getting closer to perfection. Nothing was more rewarding than seeing the numbers go down on the scale. I noticed men paying more attention to me, and women were jealous of my trim figure and popularity. That gave me power.

"But it took tremendous discipline to maintain my figure. I exercised in my room for hours, then I went running, and I ate very little. I started dating a guy, and I tried to hide my exercise and eating habits from him because they made me feel vulnerable. He found out eventually and tried to get me to relax, but it was too much pressure for me, and we split up. I'm focused again on my exercise and food routines. I have a wonderful social life, but people can't imagine *how pressured, restricted, and unhappy I always feel* trying to maintain a perfect body."

BEAUTY IS IN THE EYE OF THE VIEWER [5]

Carol's story may sound familiar because women around the world face enormous pressures and expectations related to appearance, based on their culture's norms and ideals of beauty. What is considered "beautiful" varies across the globe, but there are some common ideals, such as looking youthful.[6]

In addition to the pressures of cultural beauty norms, we are bombarded constantly by the media's ideals of beauty (often influenced heavily by Western culture), which are generally unrealistic and unattainable for the majority of women. Living up to these ideals is connected with being accepted, successful, and popular; and with finding love and belonging. This leads to social pressure to strive for these ideals. Women may feel they need to look a certain way to be attractive to other men or women, to be admired by a potential romantic partner, or to fit in. Typical thoughts along these lines are: *"If only I looked more like my friend, maybe this guy I've met would be interested in me."* Or, *"If I weighed less, I would look more professional and get the promotion I've been working toward."*

Beauty can be a definite asset in life, just like being intelligent or having a friendly personality. Beautiful people are pleasant to the eye and likely to be considered good people, which can attract both professional and personal interest from others—benefits that can lead to connections and possibilities for a better life.[7] But physical appearances are fleeting, and interest or attraction based solely on prettiness eventually fades if other, more deeply attractive qualities, do not complement it. *On its own, beauty can be a problem if it becomes the single objective and focus of life.*

THE HOLY GRAIL OF YOUTH

Women of all ages may also feel pressure to retain a youthful image for as long as possible, regardless of the risks or costs involved. This can lead women into adverse circumstances, such as eating disorders, plastic surgery damage, excessive spending, and the psychological distress that comes from thinking that self-worth and opportunities are derived mainly from physical appearance.

THE WEIGHT OF WORTHINESS

The pressure to be the ideal weight is one of the most robust and widespread appearance-related pressures women experience. In many cultures, being the "ideal weight" means being thin, and being thin is linked with perceptions of receiving appreciation and approval from others. Any weight that is not "thin" may be perceived as "overweight" and associated with negative personality traits, such as laziness or lack of discipline, for which the person is blamed and shamed. At the same time, it is not enough to just be thin: women should be lean, with muscle tone and perfect curves in all the right places.

PRESSURE COOKER

The pressure to be beautiful, thin, and young is associated with other stresses women suffer, like constantly monitoring their body.[8] Also, these pressures are the foundation of other expectations placed on women. For example, women may hear that they will *not be able to find a partner or get married* unless they maintain their looks. A woman who is doing well in her career and personal life but is considered overweight may believe that if she could lose weight, she would really *have it all* and be her "best self." Women feel much pressure to be perfect or at least to present themselves flawlessly. Veering from societal expectations for beauty, youth, and thinness *violates this quest for perfection.*

WHERE DO BODY IMAGE PRESSURES COME FROM?

Let's zero in on the body image ideal of being thin and where some of this pressure comes from. Body image has become a *central characteristic* in our culture.[9] External appearance is the first thing we notice when we meet someone, and we begin making inferences about a person's psychological traits and characteristics within a few minutes of meeting him or her.[10] For example, slimness is often associated with being disciplined and energetic, while being overweight is connected with laziness and lack of drive.

The media is the leading proponent of unrealistic beauty and body image ideals. The internet has given people all over the world—at increasingly younger ages—unprecedented access to a wide variety of media platforms. Media is often driven by "news" about the inner workings of celebrity culture, which not only glamorizes unattainable standards of beauty but also *connects appearance with success.*

The internet also allows us to present ourselves as we would like others to see us. Take online dating, for example, where it is common for women to post pictures that make them look younger or thinner or to give "alternative facts" regarding their weight and age to portray a "more attractive" image and get more swipes and likes. Some people say they are simply putting their best foot forward using all the tools available or that understating their weight based on their ideal goal "motivates" them. Sadly, what really underlies these behaviors is feelings of *body dissatisfaction*, that we are not good enough as we are, and that being loved and appreciated are conditional on looking a certain way.

Family environments, where children are socialized on the norms and expectations of their culture, are another source of pressure.

Parents and relatives may have fixed ideas of what standards and goals their daughters need to reach to have a "perfect life," and children readily internalize these ideals. Considering that they come from people children are raised to love, trust, and depend on for their well-being strengthens the tendency to perpetuate this pressure.

Peer influence is powerful. It adds to family social pressures and exposure to the media, as children and youth try to live up to their role models and forge their own identity. They may feel the need to be popular to access opportunities: and to be popular, they need to be good-looking, which is often equated with being the "right" weight.

To be overweight is a kind of failure in our society because people often believe it is the result of an individual's choices. It is different from being short or having a particular ethnic background or sexual orientation—characteristics or identities in which the person does not have an active role. However, if you are overweight, it is because of your actions: overeating, not being proactive, being lazy, not caring, and so on, so the wrongly drawn conclusion is that *your weight must be a reflection of who you are.* We are no longer looking at just a person's physical shape; we are beginning to make assumptions about their character and potential without considering practical realities, such as genetics and health.

On the other hand, society rewards women who are beautiful, slim, and youthful-looking. These women are more likely to be popular and sought out in social and professional situations. This has *a reinforcing effect and creates a cycle*: the thinner and more good-looking you are, the more you feel accepted and wanted, and the more effort, energy, and resources you put into maintaining your appearance and controlling your weight, so you continue to get that positive feedback.

In searching for acceptance and appreciation, women of all ages may work hard to try to "control" their bodies in conformity with society's expectations. As a consequence, they may develop an obsession with *monitoring their weight and modifying their appearance*. We equate this with demonstrating willpower and fighting indulgence.

However, this self-monitoring often leaves women with low self-esteem, which is especially detrimental to teenagers and young women. Many women experience intense dissatisfaction with their body and stress about their eating habits because they are struggling to lose weight, trying hard to maintain a lower weight, or feel that eating is the "one enjoyable thing" they have in life.

Note that even though body dissatisfaction is unpleasant, if the feelings are channeled healthily, they can be turned toward positive outcomes: better nutrition and exercise habits, improved relationship with self, and, if necessary, weight loss.

The pressure to be thin is linked to increased risk of developing eating disorders, which are harmful at any age, but especially so for children, when healthy physical development is so important. Based on societal feedback, the internalized ideal body image is compared—realistically or not—to one's appearance. The result can be body image dissatisfaction, which is linked to *disordered eating*.

Ashley's story shows how social pressures about physical appearance can affect women over the long-term.

"At 13, my weight was average, but I wanted to be thinner, like the popular girls in school. I had the idea—maybe because my mom was a little overweight—that I needed to be slim to have a great life and opportunities. My parents were having a lot of problems, and my mom accused my dad of having an affair. I figured my dad was looking at other women because my mom was overweight.

"I was on my own a lot, and my family's problems were starting to affect my social interactions. My friends thought I was quieter, less funny, and stopped hanging out with me. I believed if I lost weight, it might help me to feel better about myself and make new friends. My weight began to drop, and my peers commented on this. I felt so great being recognized and appreciated.

"The more weight I lost, the less I ate. Sometimes I just forgot about food. Occasionally, I was hungry and ate and then purged in secret. Nobody knew what I was doing. I felt good about my body. *Boys asked me for dates, girls asked me for tips.* It really gave me a sense of accomplishment. Everything was on the up and up: I was disciplined with my diet, I looked great in all my clothes, I made new friends and became popular. But *I started having some problems*: my period stopped, and I began to feel tired all the time, depressed, and worried about little things. My parents began to notice and became concerned but couldn't agree on how to help me. I stopped eating meals with them and stayed in my room when I was home.

"One day, I didn't feel well. I didn't tell my parents and went to school anyway. Shortly after, I felt worse, and then everything stopped. I woke up in the hospital and was told that I had passed out. This was a turning point for me, the start of a long and complicated treatment process to recover from an eating disorder.

"I'm twenty-five now, and I still have problems related to eating and food. I'm afraid I won't ever really feel happy again, but I try to keep up with my treatment plan so I can regain my health. I want to have a career and live my life. *I don't want to be trapped in this unrealistic situation where all my future hopes and expectations are linked to having a perfect body.*

"I don't want to be obsessive about my weight and appearance; but at the same time, I'm concerned about losing control of my body and becoming overweight like my mother and being rejected. It's a terrible dilemma that makes my life miserable, and I don't know how to resolve it. I'm still in recovery."

Even when women have reached their ideal weight, many struggle to maintain it and fear losing the sense of self-worth and control achieved through weight loss. We begin to see food, not as fuel for life and a source of drive and vitality, but as caloric numbers we must struggle with and regulate to obtain and maintain a perfect figure.

Consider how many celebrations, holidays, and special events are linked to preparing and eating food. Instead of these events being a source of joy and togetherness, our focus may be on how they might *ruin our progress or hinder our goals*. Then we feel guilty about this internal struggle and inability to take pleasure at the moment.

Anne, an MBA graduate student, exemplifies this point: "I think about how nice it would be to eat freely at a party. *In my case, it's not possible.* I'm afraid to lose control or gain weight again, which I hate. I usually have to give excuses. I say I have food allergies or that I'm vegan. If I eat something that's not in my diet, I purge afterward, which is a problem in social situations. I have to find a bathroom and be sure I'm not heard. Or I'll reduce my food intake to a minimum to compensate for eating the wrong thing. This makes parties and holidays less fun. The same happens on trips, where part of the adventure is trying different foods, but it's not possible for me."

Gloria shared her experience of how being pressured to be thin and look a certain way affected her life: "I was overweight as a child and preteen, but I didn't think of it as a negative then. People often told me I was cute. But by the time I was 14, I started feeling like an outsider. All the girls and women I saw on TV and social media had absolutely perfect bodies and faces. I looked at myself in the mirror, and what I saw was a chubby face and overweight body, unattractive to me and everyone else. I couldn't fit into any cool clothes, and nobody asked me out.

"My parents wondered how to help me. They were worried, especially my mom—but when I look back on her approach, I think *she hurt me more than helped.* She said it would be difficult, if not impossible, for me to have a happy life if I couldn't find a good husband, and the way to find the right guy was to have a perfect body.

"Throughout the rest of my teen years, my social life was nonexistent. The more my parents pressured me to lose weight and hang out with friends, the more I wanted to do the opposite of what they said to try to maintain some autonomy. If they hadn't pressured me so much, I think I would have figured out how to be okay. But eventually, *food became the only thing I had.* After eating, I hated myself and promised to change. My binges became more severe and secret. I was ashamed of them, but they were also the only thing that gave me a sense of gratification.

"I started lying about my weight, apologizing for it, or trying to show that I was okay with my body as it was. The truth is, I was ashamed of my body, and *the pressure to be thin made things worse.* I was so far away from the expected ideal that I felt, *why try anymore?* My self-esteem was so low I didn't think I could do anything to change.

"Once I spent two days asleep, and when I woke up, I started thinking about *how a single aspect of my life was destroying my happiness.* It was a wakeup call for me, and I started putting my energies into developing other aspects of myself that had nothing to do with weight. Gradually, as I built myself up, I was able to come back to the issue of my weight and take positive action to eat well and exercise. I really love my body now."

REFLECTIONS:
YOUR APPEARANCE IS NOT WHO YOU ARE

There is no one perfect body or ideal life. Your appearance is not who you are. Anyone who tells you otherwise is creating unrealistic expectations, which always come with stress, unhappiness, and problems. *Your body is yours—private and precious.* It is one of the most important parts of yourself to protect from outside interference, the expectations of others, and the conditioning of societal norms. Unlearning patterns and ideas that do not contribute to our personal growth and fulfillment is a way *to release tension and create space for new, healthier ideas and behaviors.* It can be challenging work, but it is worth it.

Take some time to think about your personal ideas and opinions regarding beauty and pathways to success and popularity. Ask yourself, *"Where does this idea come from? What is the story behind this feeling or this ideal?"* Maybe you will recognize the influences of cultural expectations, family upbringing, societal pressures, personal experiences, or things you have heard from other women.

The point is to notice whether some of the things that feel like "you" may actually be messages you learned from other sources and internalized. If so, *are they helpful or harmful? Is it time to let them go?*

3

The Pressure to Be Perfect

Anne, the daughter of farmers, asked her parents if she could go to college. "Yes," they told her, "you can go—but just for one year, and if you don't do well, you'll have to return to the farm." The message Anne heard from her parents was: *it's okay to try something new, provided you do it correctly from the beginning.*

Anne's story is not unique. You may know from personal experience that women and girls are expected not only to look "right" but also to act "right"—*to be perfect.* From a young age, there is a lot of pressure on girls to play safely, be careful, and not do anything risky. This continues as girls grow into women with pressure to plan carefully, to be cautious, to act appropriately, and to do things flawlessly from the start—or not at all.

This pressure is particularly intense when a woman attempts something that goes beyond the lifestyle or career choices typically associated with women and femininity. The thinking is: a woman should not bother trying to do something different unless she can do it "right." *Taking risks, whether in life, a career, or even in play and personal endeavors, is not considered feminine.*

The expectation of perfection comes from many sources, including parents, teachers, partners, coworkers, the media, and religion. Social expectations become personal expectations as women *internalize* the messages and models they are exposed to. This creates a vicious cycle: unrealistic societal expectations pressure women to live in ways that are impossible to maintain and lead to tremendous stress and tension.

Nonetheless, we keep trying because when we act following the pressure to be perfect, we are rewarded with acceptance, inclusion, and recognition that we are "real women." This keeps us striving for unattainable and unsustainable perfection, even when it results in a shrinkage of our authentic selves to fit into the box that society or family has created for us, or when it leads to crippling self-doubt and lack of confidence about our worth and capabilities.

SOCIETY'S "PERFECTION" MESSAGING TO WOMEN

Some of the messages women receive consistently from their families and communities include:

- *People's opinions of you are essential. Be a good, gracious woman so that others will like you.*
- *Make decisions that align with others' expectations; do not rock the boat and create trouble for others or yourself.*
- *If you're not sure what to do, don't do anything. Taking risks can lead to mistakes, which will affect others' opinions of you.*

These attitudes and messages, whether implied or direct, are affecting girls and women. Some studies show increased psychological maladjustment linked to misperceiving common goals as unattainable accomplishments because of the pressure to be, act, and look perfect.[11]

There are gender-typed differences in how boys (and men) and girls (and women) are socialized.[12] When boys face a problem, they are expected to analyze the situation and work out a solution themselves. When girls come up against a challenge, everyone jumps in with advice or tries to resolve the issue for her—with feedback that she is not in control or that finding the "right guy" will make her life a lot easier.

THE RISKS OF STRIVING FOR PERFECTION

What are the problems that come with continually striving for perfection? One of the biggest dangers is the *loss of creativity*. Being creative is an avenue not only for learning but also for joy. If women are not given the opportunity to practice and think creatively, to try and fail without fear, how can we achieve the learning and growth that enable us to reach our goals? Failure is necessary for progress. When we fail, we ask different and better questions; we restructure, we start again, we try something new. Failure is a tremendous opportunity for personal development. Evolving requires taking risks, making mistakes, learning from them, and going beyond our comfort zone. This involves recognizing, confronting, and disregarding the pressure to be perfect.

When we focus on perfection, we miss the growth and discoveries that are implicit in trial and error—a fundamental way of finding new solutions and opportunities. We lose out on the *character-building development* that comes with practicing determination, purpose, persistence, and endurance in the pursuit of a goal. We bypass opportunities to test our capabilities and learn how strong we really are.

Think about this: If we aim to do things perfectly, we will be looking at and following external signs of success—*Do other people like it? Do other people like me?*—instead of concentrating on our inner development and personal progress: *How am I growing through this process? What have I learned? Do I enjoy this?*

If we do not experience persevering toward a goal, we can miss the substantial benefits that come from *contact with reality*. Most of the time, the reality of a situation is not as bad as our thoughts and feelings make it out to be. When we confront a scary situation and face our fears, we often find that the situation is not as challenging as our worries or critics made us feel, that we have resources to deal with it, or that it represents an opportunity for new possibilities. Facing reality awakens our resilience: *What resources do I have to manage this situation? How can I overcome? Is a growth opportunity there for me?*

The story of Rebecca, an attractive Latin American woman, is an illustration: "A few years into my marriage, my husband started to come home later and later every day, but he always had reasons that sounded valid. Eventually I realized he was seeing another woman, but I kept on as if everything were okay. In my culture, women show 'strength' by maintaining the family together no matter what. I was scared of ending my marriage and people thinking I was a failure, so I kept trying to maintain our 'relationship,' but he was more and more distant, and I was increasingly distressed.

"One day I realized I had waited and suffered enough, and I had nothing to lose by talking with him about the situation. So I did, and he confessed that he was in love with another woman. What I felt was a relief, because now we could make a change. I found that I wasn't worried about ending my marriage. Instead, *I felt courageous and brave for facing reality*; I felt strong when I considered the possibilities ahead, even though I was going against societal expectations. It was a tough journey, but I'm happy with myself for choosing the path that was right for me."

The mind has a way of magnifying challenges with worries and fears. The longer we give worry the driver's seat, the harder the problem becomes, and the weaker we feel. However, when we are honest about our reality and take action, we find that the challenges are manageable, that we are capable—and we become stronger.

PRESSURE TO BE PERFECT LEADS TO FEELING JUDGMENT, SHAME, AND GUILT

Unfortunately, Rebecca's experience is not that common. Many women do not give themselves the opportunity to be real about their situations, deal with their circumstances honestly, and grow from the journey. They feel pressured to present *a perfect façade* and get things right on the first try. When things go wrong, they feel inadequate, that they are not good enough or have not tried their best, which leads to self-doubt. If we are not "good enough," we feel shame, that there is something wrong with us. If we have not done our best, we feel guilty that our actions are wrong or inefficient.[13] Feeling shame and guilt can be a general negative sensation or linked to a particular situation in our lives: home life, work, or specific relationships with a partner, child, or parent.

This provides a partial explanation of why some women put up with domestic violence: they have internalized the message that they are not good enough or not doing their best and think the abuse happens as a consequence of it.[13,14] Related to this is the responsibility, and often accompanying shame or guilt, women feel *to build a better relationship or change a bad one.* Women are socialized to be the caregivers, the nurturers, and to develop an understanding of feelings. As a result, when a relationship is going poorly, women (especially in conservative environments) are more likely to take the blame and bear the brunt of "fixing" it or holding things together.[13,14]

AM I 'GOOD ENOUGH'?

Feeling inadequate, that we are "not good enough," is one of the deepest, most painful human fears. Women are under continuous pressure "to have it all"—to embody and demonstrate perfection. If a woman has a happy family life and prosperous career but is overweight or not very sociable, others will perceive *something wrong* with her. Such judgments are based on subjective opinions by people who rarely see the full picture of a woman's life.

Helen, a woman in her early twenties, shared with me her feelings about not being good enough: "When I was a teenager, I started to think there was something wrong with me. Nothing my parents suggested interested me, and none of my interests were adequate for them. They made it clear I had to be more feminine, that the activities I liked weren't acceptable for young ladies. I think they didn't care about my personality or what I wanted.

"I aspired to be a good person, so I began focusing on what my parents and our church considered good: preparing myself for a profession, getting married, and having a family. But on the inside, I was worried. I wasn't good enough according to my parents' expectations, but because I wasn't pursuing what motivated me, *I also felt not good enough for me.*"

As Helen experienced, the pressure to be perfect is internalized and leads to feelings of self-doubt. If someone thinks she is "not good enough," she may also feel devalued, judged, and excluded. To avoid these painful feelings and subsequent low self-esteem and self-confidence, she may imitate external behaviors associated with success.

In general, boys and men are not subjected to the same pressures to be perfect that women experience. They are socialized and encouraged—in fact, expected—to take risks and be decisive. They are told *it is okay to be "good enough" just to get to the next step,* which provides space to grow and to enjoy the process. Women need to hear this type of messaging too.

Joyce explained the struggles she faced in trying to navigate her career and deal with pressures to be perfect: "I've been with my company for ten years, in the same position, with similar tasks and responsibilities. I've had some opportunities to apply for higher-level jobs in the company, but I didn't take them because I'm afraid of messing up and being judged by my peers and my boss. I'm operating in my comfort zone, so I'm not making mistakes, but maybe I'm also not making progress.

"Over the years, many of my coworkers have gotten better positions and salaries. I don't know how to do that. I'm afraid I'll be seen as aggressive and selfish if I pursue an opportunity for improvement. Besides, how will I perform in situations I don't know well? I'm good at what's familiar to me, but in new circumstances, people who matter are going to see my flaws and that I'm not good enough. *My quality of life is suffering because I'm trying to live up to this expectation of perfection.* I try to copy what I see some other women doing and be more assertive or articulate, but I worry about acting in a way that isn't authentically me.

"The same thing happens in my relationship with my boyfriend. We've been together for years, and our life is all about routine—the same activities, the same conversations, the same ways of doing things, again and again. I'm okay in our comfort zone, but I'm afraid he'll get bored with our life together and leave me. I don't know what's worse: to try to change and let him see it's a struggle for me or to continue with this stagnant life."

REFLECTIONS: IT IS IMPOSSIBLE TO BE FLAWLESS FROM THE GET-GO

It is healthy to set goals and challenge ourselves to go beyond our comfort zone. However, we do ourselves a disservice when we try to meet the impossible, unrealistic objective of being flawless from the get-go. We need to allow ourselves time, possibilities for creativity, and the space for learning that comes with trial and error. That way, we can experience the evolution that arises from going outside our comfort zone.

Instead of aiming for perfection, *focus your attention and efforts on making progress, learning, and building resilience.* Take pride in the personal growth your hard work makes possible. Do not worry about being liked or others' opinion of you. *Trust yourself and your journey.* As you grow personally, you are going to discover even more beautiful, worthy parts of yourself.

Mistakes and failures are an inevitable part of the growth process; learn to see them as evidence that you have acted with bravery and courage. Changing your perspective on stepping outside your comfort zone and making mistakes will help you build self-esteem, a driving force for continued growth.

As you take this high road, you are going to encounter others like you who are also seeking personal growth over popularity, looking perfect, or avoiding judgment. Seize the opportunity to live the life you want and deserve.

4

The Pressure to Be Subordinate

For two years, Emily and her husband Edgar worked together after hours and on weekends to build an online software company from the ground up. Once it finally took off, their business performed so well they were both able to quit their day jobs and focus on their startup. Slowly, Emily began to realize she was taking on all the clerical and behind-the-scenes roles while Edgar made the big trips and presented as the face of the business—because it was "beneficial to the company's image to have a man taking the lead."

Sharon's husband was the CEO of a big company. His business partners and potential clients frequently visited their home, where Sharon was expected to be a gracious hostess, wife, and mother. Once all of the kids were in school, Sharon wanted to return to school herself to build her career prospects, but her husband was adamantly against this idea. He said they needed "stability" in their home life to sustain his career. How could he maintain his public image and entertain guests if Sharon was "off somewhere" instead of attending to the household?

If you have a story like Emily's or Sharon's, you are not alone. They were both experiencing a type of pressure that many women worldwide have felt, whether in their private, professional, or social lives: the expectation that a woman's place is to be subordinate—to play a supporting or dependent role—to the man (or men) in her life. In my opinion, this is *the linchpin social pressure women face*, and it derives from a male-dominated ideology rather than a real assessment of women's aptitudes and capabilities.

AT THE ROOT: PATRIARCHY

Patriarchy as a system is informed and maintained by male-centered ideologies that concentrate power and control in the hands of men (specifically those demonstrating masculinity) and create unequal social structures for women.[15] The subordination of women is part of this social system. *Women are expected to take second place behind men, and men are to give women protection, identity, and a role.*

The socialization that maintains this patriarchal norm begins early in life: boys are oriented to take part in sports, to be assertive, to develop competencies and interests. Girls are socialized to play with dolls, to interact "nicely" with others, and to build the capacity to be obedient, pleasant, nurturing companions.

THE IMPACT ON WOMEN'S PROFESSIONAL LIVES

This socialization follows from private life into public and professional spheres, where women are more likely (often expected) to take on "helping" jobs as assistants or secretaries. If a woman has a leading role, it may be assumed a man helped her get there. Or the woman is expected to have double or triple the competencies and experience of her male counterparts to be eligible to compete for positions. Even when women have similar or higher-level education and capabilities as compared to their male counterparts, they have to work harder to gain the equivalent trust and respect.

In Emily's case, Edgar assumed she would be happy with an assistant role because it meant handling easier, less challenging tasks. "When I said I wanted more," Emily told me, "people's reaction was, *'What's wrong with you?'* Like I was ungrateful. What was 'wrong' was that I wanted my place in the company, to be the co-leader with my husband, not to be in second place."

As a result of this situation at work, Emily and Edgar's relationship became strained. Emily felt torn, not only because almost all the employees, men and women, took Edgar's side, but also because she thought their children responded as though she was creating conflict. "I had two options," Emily said, "either keep fighting for my rightful place or accept the second-place role. For the success of our company, for our marriage to have a future, and for our children, I accepted that second place. *Everybody was happy, except me. I felt miserable.*"

WOMEN EXCLUDED FROM POSITIONS OF POWER

Men retaining positions of power and women being obstructed from even seeking—much more holding—positions of power is central to the pressure on women to be dependent or subordinate. Women may be allowed to maintain some semblance of control in limited circumstances, such as certain particulars of domestic life. But then again, Emily's experience highlights the sense of *surprise or sus-*

picion that is common when a woman wants or takes on a visible position of power, especially in business or politics. Being interested in power is not "feminine." Many people will see her ambition as an indication of some "problem" in her life, which they believe they have free rein to criticize: *"She's so aggressive and controlling." "Maybe she couldn't find a partner." "She must not care that much about her family."*

Women have to work extra hard to inspire trust in their abilities. Due to the expectations of perfection that surround women, female leaders are more likely to be blamed and judged when things go wrong. Women's mistakes are seen as proof of their "weak, emotional character," an inherent "flaw." By contrast, because male leaders come with less "expectations baggage," their errors are more likely to be forgiven, and their mistakes are seen as one-off incidents that are soon forgotten.

Women also contribute to this pressure to play a secondary, supporting role when they criticize other women who are working hard to get ahead for trying to go beyond their "natural station." The influence of patriarchal systems is so strong in our society that trailblazing women often pay the price on both sides of the path.

The subordination of women can also be seen in patriarchal religious systems where leadership and authority are concentrated in the hands of men, and women are relegated to secondary positions where they are not permitted to perform spiritual or management functions, limiting their participation and influence.

PRESSURE COOKER

The pressure to be perfect raises its ugly head and combines with the pressure to be subordinate or dependent in several ways:

Dependence and the
need to be liked

Women are raised to think they need to be liked to succeed in their personal and professional lives; and to be liked, they need to be feminine, neither too demanding nor aggressive. Fear of rejection—whether in negotiating a salary or pay raise, or asking someone out—is a dominant force that keeps women in traditional gender roles, *hesitant to go beyond the bounds of the few possibilities presented to them*. Women who are bold, ambitious, courageous, and creative are going against the grain of society's expectations. They challenge the pressure to be perfect and the pressure to be dependent.

Dependence and
fear of failure

In many cases, the "power" women have is limited to accepting or refusing someone or something offered rather than real power to pursue whatever they want, especially when *it involves taking a risk*. The pressure to be perfect kills creativity and can lead to stagnation in our development because it removes the chance to learn from our failures and grow through pursuing our goals. Taking risks, practicing creativity, and learning from trial and error build endurance and open the door to exponential personal development.

Dependence and unhealthy comfort zones

There is a subtle, dangerous reinforcement pattern that occurs when a woman yields to societal pressure to accept a second-place role: *"If I act according to the expectation that I'll be submissive and dependent, in exchange, I'll receive protection, care, and approval. These are things I want in my life, but will this avenue of accepting them create a comfort zone that's negative for my personal growth? However, if I try to resist this pressure, I'll run into conflict and questions."* Mothers frequently advise their daughters to avoid conflict and be grateful for the attention and care they receive by accepting that second-place and a comfort zone.

"From the beginning of our marriage, my husband didn't want me to return to school or get a job outside his family business. So I was a housewife and worked for him through the ups and downs of his business. It was a good deal for him but not for me. I'm not at all interested in his field. He's the kind of person who evaluates people based on what they bring to the table. In his opinion and mine, I don't bring much; I'm just an extension of him. In some ways, maybe he's right since I do what's expected of me without personal motivation. I'm getting older now, and I don't feel I have other options. That increases my dependency on him, and I feel he values me less because I don't have more skills. *Sometimes he doesn't respond when I talk to him, or he makes belittling comments about what I say.* I wanted to be a good wife and make him feel he was a priority to me. Some days I cry in the bathroom and wonder how this happened. I just feel so tired and unhappy."—*Cynthia*

LACK OF VALIDATION

The pressure on women to be subordinate and dependent is often linked with a lack of validation of who they are and their inherent self-worth. It can even lead to humiliation and abuse, as in Katherine's story:

"When we decided to marry, I quit my job and moved to the city where my husband lived. From the beginning of our relationship, he's been in charge. He tells me how he wants me to act. He decides what we eat, how I dress, when we have sex, what we're doing on weekends and vacations. I try not to contradict him because he has a short temper and gets frustrated. If I disagree, he explodes. Then he attempts to repair the damage, holds my hand, promises not to do it again, and the cycle starts over. At the same time, he's a responsible provider, we lack for nothing, and his family members, coworkers, and friends appreciate him.

"I don't have scheduling obligations like my husband and children, so my time is not relevant. I feel the only time my work around the house is noticed is if something isn't done correctly. *I live in the shadow of my husband, trying to hide the negatives of our relationship.* I'm ashamed of the humiliations I tolerate, but sometimes I think I deserve them. I have a secret: sometimes when I'm alone at home, I drink a lot. I don't think it's right, but it's the only time I feel some comfort."

REFLECTIONS: CREATING SPACE FOR A HEALTHY GIVE-AND-TAKE

As children, we are vulnerable and have to depend on others for survival. Nevertheless, as we grow up, we need to develop the confidence, personal independence, and sense of self-worth that *empower us to have equality in relationships.*

There are three keys to rising above this pressure to be dependent:
- Developing confidence that you are enough
- Establishing economic independence
- Becoming aware of power dynamics in relationships

Whatever your situation is right now, I encourage you to build personal self-sufficiency in your life. Permit yourself to try new things, to learn more about your preferences, strengths, and areas for growth. This will help you develop confidence in your abilities to take care of yourself, to make decisions that are right, and to find solutions to challenges.

Additionally, it is crucial to invest in your career and grow your professional competencies—this is always worthy because it will increase your confidence and give you the tools for economic independence, which will allow you greater latitude for self-determination in your personal life.

Power imbalances are prevalent in relationships, but remember that it takes two people to create relational power. Whether in intimate relationships, with friends, family, or in the workplace, you want to create space for respectful, considerate give-and-take. Sometimes you will take the lead and have more influence; at other times, you will play a supporting role. Communication is key to the process of developing a healthy partnership and relational power.

If someone is putting you down, trying to win at any cost, or treating you disrespectfully, the relational power dynamic is imbalanced and probably causing harm. An essential part of self-care is recognizing that you have power and then using it—*caring for yourself should be your top priority.*

As you can see, we can make changes in our internal perspective as well as in our behavior to consolidate our power and experience happiness and success.

5

The Pressure to Get Married

At Kelly's twenty-ninth birthday, the question everyone asked her was: "When are you going to find a man and settle down?" "As if I know!" Kelly later told me. *Everyone had something to say about the fact that I'm not in a long-term relationship right now. I would like to have a partner eventually, but I'm happy with my life as it is and being on my own. I have much freedom to come and go as I want.*

Over the last decades, we have seen many changes in American culture and societal norms when it comes to marriage. For example, women are getting married later, at twenty-seven years of age on average.[16] Nonetheless, half of the American adults are married,[17] and women between the ages of twenty-five and thirty-five experience much pressure to find a life partner. In other countries and cultures, women experience this pressure to get married with higher intensity and at younger ages.[18] You may have felt this societal expectation firsthand in your own life, as though there was no other acceptable life choice for women.

In many parts of the world and for generations, marriage has been used to limit women's choices and possibilities. Here are some examples:

- According to patriarchal gender norms, being a mother is perceived to be the essential goal and vital manifestation of womanhood—a woman's destiny. In many cultures, marriage is the prerequisite to motherhood.[19]

- Patriarchal ideology implies that women are childishly helpless and inherently weak, so they require continual oversight and support of either their immediate family or a husband. Marriage is a rite of passage, a sign of entering adulthood. However, a woman cannot achieve independence from her parents on her own; it is necessary to find a man who cares for and protects her. Only then the family is willing to let her go—not because they trust her as a person, but because there is now someone else to look after her.[19]

While marriages based on love and personal intimacy are more the norm today, patriarchal structures still underlie society's expectations for a woman: that *by a certain society-dictated age, she will have a life partner, become a mother, and so on.* Marriage symbolizes an ideal goal for women: it is the happy ending wherein a woman finds her perfect match, who will love, care for, and protect her. It is the beginning of every other aspect of a woman's "destiny" and expected accomplishments. If a woman veers from this path, she is likely to be on the receiving end of concern, disappointment, unwelcome jokes, and rude comments. She may be underappreciated and seen as less valuable. Women in these situations can internalize these tensions, and they feel not only external but also self-generated pressures.

Consequently, as you may know from your own experience or that of friends, finding a suitable spouse or partner is a priority for many women. Nevertheless, not all women are interested, and not all interested women find an opportunity, which may lead to the following:
- Women who choose to be single
- Women who want to get married or have a partner but cannot find "the one"

Women who choose to be single

It is one thing to want to be single and live independently, but it is another to choose to be single in a world that idealizes coupled life. Singleness is commonly associated with unhappiness, vulnerability (that is, you are alone), a difficult personality, and loss of the emotions and exciting moments that can be shared "only" with a partner, such as building a home, raising children, experiencing couple or family activities.

Remember, too, that gender norms in a patriarchal system suggest that the universal dream of girls is *to grow up longing for a white wedding dress and a handsome prince with whom to ride off into the sunset.* So if you choose a single life and give up all the marvelous things popular culture links with marriage, people—especially those closest to you—are probably going to be surprised.

Following is a summary of my conversations with Pamela, a thirty-three-year-old woman, about the pressures she experienced regarding her decision to remain single:

"Growing up, I realized that getting married, or finding a partner, was what society expected of women. I prefer to be by myself. I've had several boyfriends, and I was happier with some than others, but in general, I'm not comfortable with sharing space, so being together over weekends or on vacations was tough. I always felt more like myself when these relationships ended. Friends and family think I'm shy, but I'm not. I do pretty well in most social circumstances and meeting new people. But to be truly comfortable with myself, I need to live alone.

"I have no trouble talking about this. The problem is hearing the comments that are going on behind my back. Some of my loved ones are uneasy about my choices. I tell them that being single is based on my personal preferences at this time. I'm alone but not lonely. That's when the criticism starts about me not having feelings, being empty, or not knowing what I'm missing. Some people think I must have been hurt, so I don't trust men, or that I'm insecure or afraid to get hurt. *I tell them again that being single is a personal decision, and they look at me with sadness and suggest I'll be unhappy forever.* Sometimes I hear that I'm single because my standards are too high. But there's nothing wrong with having high standards for a life partner."

Women who want to get married or have a partner but cannot find "the one"

Many women are disappointed with their love life, and they often blame themselves: *"What am I doing wrong?"* Especially when women are in their late twenties and thirties, they may have personal expectations related to intimacy and receive negative societal messages that denigrate being "alone."

These personal expectations and societal messages are informed by each other in a cycle that positions single life as an undesirable state that necessitates change, self-improvement, explaining your situation to others, and trying continually to "put yourself out there."

As we all know, establishing a relationship can be difficult. First, it involves two people, one of whom you cannot control. Second, especially in the twenty-to-thirty age bracket, people are still figuring out what they want to do and be in life. One person may hope to get married right away, while the other might not be ready for a serious relationship. One person may be hesitant to commit, while the other may worry that her partner might vanish suddenly and cause her pain. People may be afraid of making the wrong choice: *"How can I be sure he's the right one for me?"*

There is often anxiety *not to miss the boat.* In that case, a woman might seem desperate to settle down, which may be a turnoff to her potential partner. This anxiety may also complicate a relationship if one person thinks the other's interest is based on trying to find a spouse as quickly as possible, rather than on genuine interest.

Denise, an attractive woman in her forties, asked me: "What do I have to do if I want a relationship? I've smiled constantly, laughed at any bit of fun, acted pleased, and was extremely nice. I've done all of this, and nothing has happened. I think I'll be single forever. I haven't had a relationship with real future. *Maybe I look so desperate that guys run away.*"

SOCIETY'S VIEW OF SINGLE WOMEN

Instead of valuing and appreciating single women, society and the media depict them in cruel terms: If they are young, they may be called "*piranhas*" who want to take on married men. If they are older and interested in a younger partner, they are "*cougars.*" A "*spinster*" is an older, unmarried woman associated with the "crazy cat lady" stereotype.

In my conversations with single women in the United States and other countries, I found that, in general, they did not expect to go through life alone. Many remembered feeling sorry for aunts or family friends who were single at older ages; they thought their own experience would be different. However, the older these women got, the harder it seemed to find an appropriate partner, and *the more pressure they felt to establish a conventional life path that included marriage or an acceptable partnership.*

Beverly is a doctor and devoted a good part of her life to her studies, training, and practice. When Beverly's father died, she returned to live with her elderly, widowed mother. Gradually, a mutual dependency developed between the two women. Beverly traveled a lot for professional and personal reasons, and her mother kept the household in order, maintaining the same daily routines, which helped Beverly feel grounded after her long days of challenging work. Although their setup was harmonious, Beverly still felt much negative pressure from her social community to find a partner. She went on dates but found that the men she met were often more interested in her position or money than in herself. Beverly's mother died a few years later, and Beverly still did not have a partner, which she attributed *to "bad luck" at keeping people in her life.*

Beverly had *internalized* the tension and societal pressures of finding a partner. Rather than enjoying the circumstances she found herself in, she believed not being in a relationship was her fault. Many women experience shame ("I'm not enough") and guilt ("I didn't try hard enough") if they do not resolve the "problem" of singlehood by getting married or establishing a formal, stable partnership.

In summary, marriage, or its equivalent, is considered the *happily-ever-after ending* for all women, while the worst possible outcome is never getting married and missing the boat because opportunities or time have passed the woman by. There is a pervasive belief that all women want to get married, connected to the societal expectation that all women want to, and will, follow the same track of marriage and motherhood—in that order. All other outcomes are seen as *unexpected, incomplete, and opposite to the "ideal" way of life.*

A woman who chooses to be, or accepts being, single may experience the following:

- Direct or implicit questions from family and friends about her private life and choices

- A changing social circle, as other friends get married or start relationships
- The fear or reality of fewer eligible potential partners, as "all the good ones are taken"
- Worry about her biological clock ticking and the potential for increased risks or difficulties by delaying pregnancy
- Worry that her youth and beauty will fade as she ages, making her less attractive
- Awareness that she is on a less conventional path and feeling like the odd one out
- Assumptions that she is lonely and sad or that something is wrong with her
- Pressure to explain or justify why she is still single

These pressures and concerns ultimately connect to *feelings of loss and missing out* that become more profound and seemingly irreversible the more time passes. First, there is not having a partner, which is "essential" in our couples society. Next is the assumed inability to have a child, which is deviant from women's supposed innate purpose and destiny. Also, as the years go by, there is the increased vulnerability of being "alone." It may also be difficult to build relationships with married women because of (perceived) fewer common areas of interest. Interactions with men may be complicated, too, in that either person may be confused about reciprocal expectations. In short, many single women feel that society views them as *failures* because they are not married.[20]

Janice's story is an example:

"I feel that I'll be single forever. It's not a good feeling. What's harder is that I want to have a partner, but I seem to keep getting into bad relationships with men who don't respect me. Are all men like this? Or is it my fault? Maybe I'm sabotaging my relationships before they really get going, or maybe I look too desperate and attract the wrong guys. I keep dating because I'm already thirty-four, so *I feel a lot of pressure to figure this out.* But it's been painful, too. I lack confidence, and I don't want to get hurt again. Sometimes I dream about having a family, a home, a husband, but the reality of where my love life is today—nonexistent—makes me cry."

WHAT SINGLE WOMEN HEAR FROM THEIR INNER CIRCLE

A woman often experiences the most pressure to be in a relationship moving toward marriage from her family and close friends, those who provide the majority of her personal social support. This inner circle will frequently tell the single woman *she needs to prioritize finding a "solution" to her single status;* the longer she waits, the harder it will be to "resolve" the situation.

Some messages may be intended *to provide comfort and alleviate worries:*
- *"You're so beautiful and intelligent—any moment now, someone's going to sweep you off your feet!"*
- *"Keep trying! Don't give up! The man of your dreams is going to come."*
- *"In the future, you're going to laugh about this!"*
- *"Don't try so hard. Just be open to the universe, and the right man will come to you."*

Others messages are aimed at advising the woman on *how to "fix the problem:"*
- *"You should lose weight and buy new clothes. Spruce up your image."*
- *"Why don't you try online dating? There are a lot of opportunities there!"*

- *"You're so independent; you're scaring the men away."*
- *"You're too picky! You think nobody is good enough for you."*
- *"You don't go out enough. You have to be more social and keep meeting people to find the 'one.'"*

And I could go on! In the second set of messages, you can see an underlying thread of *blaming the woman for her single situation*. The burden is on the woman to make changes to her approach, preferences, or personality to rectify the situation.

ADDITIONAL MARRIAGE-RELATED PRESSURES IN CONSERVATIVE ENVIRONMENTS

While society in general pressures and expects women to get into a stable relationship with a man, in conservative environments, there is often an added pressure: *to be married by law and religious practices.* Living with a partner without being married is seen as a sin in many traditional religions and environments. People from ethnic minority groups, rural populations, and conservative backgrounds generally adhere to this pressure to get married as a condition to living and having an intimate relationship with someone.

Susan told me: "I'm twenty-nine and still single. My challenge is not just finding a life partner but also getting formally married according to my family and friends' expectations. I don't think a traditional marriage is what I want, but I don't know how to tell my family that. I don't want to be single forever, but I don't like the expectation that marriage is the only acceptable outcome for my life. I feel pressure from my family and friends that if I don't hurry to find a husband the opportunity will pass me by. Related to this, I'm afraid I come across as desperate for a relationship sometimes—like, *any man who shows me attention is a possible candidate, even if I don't find him attractive.* I'm not interested in getting married just to be married. But I can't blame my family for pressuring me; *they think they're acting in my best interests.* I have a good career, but for them, that's secondary to the goal of having a husband and children."

Even if a woman is in a long-term relationship, if she is not married, she is seen as incomplete, *not part of a "real" couple.* It may be assumed that this "final step" of legal and religious marriage was not taken because there is not enough love and commitment in the relationship.

Following on the heels of being married in legal and religious terms is another pressure: that *marriage is forever.* This is very explicit in religious environments especially. Divorce is not permitted: no matter what, you are stuck with your spouse. It is considered a virtue to endure a problematic relationship. Rather than the woman prioritizing her happiness, her primary obligation is maintaining the unity of her family and forgiving or forgetting whatever the problem is.

In many parts of the world, marriage-related pressures take the form of arranged marriages. They occur in a variety of ways depending on the cultural environment, but often women have no say in whether they even want to get married, let alone whom they marry. Their family decides for them, often based on community, rather than the woman's personal interest.[21]

As I mentioned, there have been many changes in recent years regarding the institution of marriage. The age at which people get married has increased, fewer couples marry, and divorce rates are rising. Nevertheless, *the pressure to get married is still a dominant force in many societies,* especially in conservative ones.

REFLECTIONS: BUILD YOUR REALITY BASED ON YOUR TRUE SELF

For thousands of years, women's lives were defined by the relationships they had with men. Women were raised to concentrate their efforts on achieving a marital relationship and to expect frustration and shame if they could not. The challenge we women still face today is to walk free from the societal notion that "nature" has laid out a single destiny for women since the beginning of time.

I encourage you to disregard the pressure to get married or find a life partner and instead put your energy into planning and doing what you need to be the person you want to be. Do not accept the path someone else has designed for you. It is a woman's right to create her destiny. What is important is what you want and who you want to be, whether you are single, married, looking for a relationship, in a long-term partnership, or something else altogether. *Be the queen of your fate—build your future according to your ideas, needs, and feelings.* You have only one life, and it is your right to develop your unique destiny according to what you want. This is not selfishness. *This is respecting your life and personal motivations.*

As you prepare yourself for what you want to be and act on your plan, you are going to find friends, tutors, and companions along the way—people who can inspire you, spark creativity, and share resources. Some of these encounters may develop into relationships that expand your being and possibilities.

Being on a path you have chosen will cause you to flourish and give you *the energy that comes from motivation and purpose.* You will find that you enjoy who you are and the life you are living. From this starting point of freedom and autonomy, you can choose, build, or fight for what you want—including whatever type of relationship you are interested in. You will transform your path from one that follows a gender-based "destiny" into a future you have made that aligns with what you like and value—*an authentic future.*

You will be amazed at how far you can go if you build your reality based on your true self instead of listening, responding to, and internalizing the expectations of others. There is no better way to develop self-worth and self-confidence than to go beyond the comfort zone established for women to an identity and goals developed through your authentic growth.

There are no stronger limits than the ones we put on ourselves. *Let them go, and live a life you love and respect yourself for.*

6

The Pressure to Have Children

Jean had been married for five years. She and her husband had a healthy, happy relationship, and Jean enjoyed her career, the home they had built together, and spontaneity in their lives and travels. But at every family gathering and social event, questions about being childless haunted her: *"Don't you want children of your own?" "What sort of woman would pick work over a child?"*

"I'm happy about my decision not to have kids," Jean told me. "But I'm frustrated that I have to keep explaining and defending my decision over and over. My family and close friends are trying to convince me that I've made a mistake by choosing to be childless; that it's not 'normal' for a woman not to have children. I feel so blessed and don't understand why people don't see the positives," Jean said. "My husband and I have so many possibilities ahead, but in my family's eyes, *we're failures because we don't want to have a child."*

This is one of the most problematic pressures faced by women because the *decision to be childless is something you have to justify, excuse, or explicate.* It does not look like a free resolution. However, it is entirely about your existence, keeping your way on a road that most people leave: the one based on your personal and your couple's identity.

Society puts women under a great deal of pressure to have children because becoming a mother is closely associated with being a "real" woman. In years past and still in many conservative environments, becoming a mother was the *inevitable destiny of women*, the only way they could become fully complete as humans—all other accomplishments were secondary.

As a result, this is one of the most challenging pressures to deal with and can lead to pain and frustration for women who do not have children, whether because of personal choice or due to other circumstances.

There are many valid reasons a woman or a couple might choose not to have children. Some partners worry that children will come between them, or cause strain and ruin their relationship. Women may fear that being a parent will slow or interrupt their escalating career. People may have concerns about the financial cost of raising a child. For others, having children reduces their ability to travel or have a certain amount of spontaneity and freedom in life. Some people have had difficult upbringings, which reduces their interest in having children of their own.

Lucy came from a dysfunctional family. Her father was an alcoholic, and her mother worked multiple shift roles to provide for the family. With her mother working long hours, Lucy, the eldest child, took on all the household responsibilities. "All my dreams were about the opposite of the type of life I was in," Lucy said. "I wanted a stable partner who shared my life choices. I wanted a good career so I would have enough money for everything I wanted, including traveling abroad."

Because all of Lucy's time went into caring for her siblings and finishing her studies, she did not have much opportunity to date in person, so she joined an online dating site. "Initially, I was really scared because of all the stories you hear about online dating going wrong. But eventually somebody contacted me, and we started talking, then dating, and we've been living together for a few years now. What I don't want in my new life is to go back to the lifestyle of my teenage years. I want to be free to focus on my career, to travel, and to enjoy doing whatever each day offers with my partner. So I don't want children. I know that this is related to how I grew up. But it's okay. *Having the freedom to make this choice is a way to overcome the negative effects of my past.* For me, the most important reason not to have children is that I like my life as it is."

Society's default expectation is that women will have children; making a different choice is still considered relatively deviant. In spite of all the progress made to advance women's rights and freedom of self-determination, society still looks down its nose at voluntary childlessness. Informing others of a decision not to have children will probably cause surprise and be followed by questions and judgment: *"How can you be sure you don't want children? How can you be so detached and self-centered?"*

Choosing to be childless opposes the stereotype of how women ought to be: thinking of others first, self-sacrificing to prioritize their needs, attending to their opinions, and not rocking the boat. Some women internalize the blame and criticism they hear and wonder whether there is *something wrong with them or with their partner or with their relationship* because they do not want to have a child.

We often consider *social and family expectations as obligations*; we see them as an indication of the "right" thing to do. In my opinion, there is almost no stronger pressure than deciding not to have children in a context and time in which it is expected that you become a mother. People seldom ask, *"Why are you a mother?"* However, they are very quick to inquire, *"Why don't you have kids?"*

The uppermost pressure to have children usually comes from a woman's family and friends who are ready to share their unsolicited advice and opinions freely. Because having children is seen as a way of adding meaning to the present and legacy to the future, guarding against loneliness, and ensuring there is someone to look after you when you are older, they will try to convince you that having children is great and how wrong you are to consider anything else.

Living a life that goes against societal expectations is difficult. You may be criticized for being selfish, narcissistic, or self-absorbed. You may be told there is something wrong with you personally or with your relationship. You may need to explain your decision repeatedly to family, friends, or other people in your life. You will probably be asked to justify how your life choices and other achievements provide you with meaningful fulfillment and satisfaction. It may be difficult to fully enjoy your lifestyle and the results of your decision when they are continually judged and misunderstood.

VOLUNTARY CHILDLESSNESS IN CONSERVATIVE ENVIRONMENTS

In many traditional rural areas, religious groups, and ethnic minority communities, personal life and family life overlap. Individual accomplishments and status are related to having a family. In these environments, the lack of a nuclear family is a sign of failure, so the decision to be childless is not an option.

"When I decided I didn't want to have kids, 90 percent of the responses I received were negative. I heard everything from *'you're selfish,' 'you'll regret it,'* and *'you aren't a real woman'* to *'God and your parents will be mad.'* Sometimes I feel that because I don't want to be a mother, *I'm perceived as an outsider to society and even to my own family.* But I made this decision years ago, based on my belief that I can't do both the things I want to do and be a mother, and I don't think I'll change. It's different for other people, but this is what's right for me. My husband and I are happy with our lives, and I have peace and joy in my decision not to have children."—*Carolyn*

SOME OF THE CHALLENGES OF DECIDING TO BE CHILDLESS

Choosing not to have children can be challenging. External pressures and messages we have internalized since childhood point toward following the "natural" order of life's milestones. The passage of time also creates enormous pressure as fertility declines with age. A woman may be unsure of what to do and worry that she will come to regret her decision not to have children, but it may be too late or too expensive to change direction.

As I mentioned, there is an underlying sense that a woman who is not a mother is less of a woman. A family of two is not really considered a "family," "just" a couple or a relationship—somehow less substantial and stable. There is an idea that childless women are not fully realized individuals and are not achieving their complete potential. The myth is that these women are or will be living an empty, lonely, self-centered life as they grow older.

Men do not experience the same degree of pressure to become a father, nor is it seen as their defining role in life. By contrast, women are guided to think about motherhood from the earliest age. When I buy toys for my nephews and nieces, it dismays me to see how gender-normed toys are, with exciting crafts- and skills-based toys for boys, and baby dolls, clothes, and kitchen sets for girls. Culture plays an active role in influencing girls' formative perspective on expectations for becoming a mother and having a family life.

Women who act in agreement with the social expectations of marriage and motherhood are seen as "good" women. Childless women have acted against expectations and are therefore "not good," "less good," or missing out on an essential life experience, which opens them up to society's judgment and blame. Feelings of *guilt and shame* are common when you do not act or respond according to others' expectations.

REFLECTIONS: FIND YOUR OWN PATH TO MEANING, SIGNIFICANCE, AND GROWTH

Becoming a mother changes a woman's present and future life significantly. Parenting is a new life role that comes with particular challenges, responsibilities, joys, risks, routines, and limitations. What occupies a woman's time, thoughts, and attention will naturally change if she becomes a mother, and as she and her family move through different phases of life. Because motherhood is such an all-encompassing, life-altering experience, it is essential that women have *absolute freedom to decide whether it is for them.*

Since choosing to be childless is the road less traveled in our society, it is crucial to have a solid foundation for your decision: one that is based on your identity as an individual and as a couple, and your goals and appeals for the future.

A fundamental component of being human is that we search for meaning and significance in life; as a result, we experience the growth that finding purpose brings.

Being a parent is an important life experience. However, *other paths also lead you to these three essential elements of life: meaning, purpose, and growth.* So the story of your future is for you to write.

7

The Pressure Not to Divorce

"I was very much in love with my husband when we married," said Linda, "and I looked forward to starting our family. Our relationship was pretty good over the first few years. Sometimes Jason was a bit distant, but I thought this was natural for a person who was used to living alone. Though it got to the point where it felt like he was hiding something, and I began to get concerned. I tried to talk to him, but he ignored me. Our relationship consisted of eating dinner silently while watching the news.

"We had two sons at this point, so I decided to give it some time and see if things changed. When they didn't, I thought I should look into divorce proceedings. I told my parents, and they were shocked. They told me it was my duty to stay with Jason, try to understand him better, and figure out how to resolve the situation. They said it was selfish of me to want a divorce, and I should instead focus on doing more family activities. *All the blame for the poor state of our marriage and the responsibility to fix things was on me.* My parents also had economic concerns, which I did too. But then there were the religious pressures, such as, 'God put you together,' and who am I to go against what God has done?"

The pressure to stay married no matter what is a strong one. Women in this situation have to deal with multiple delicate and often conflicting factors:

their own needs; their children's well-being; family opinions; and for some, religious beliefs, such as "God's will." Additionally, if a relationship is toxic, there is the risk that staying may lead to psychological and physical abuse.

If you have ever experienced this pressure while trying to figure out whether to rectify or leave an unhealthy marriage, you know how ashamed and guilty it can make you feel, even when you are not solely responsible for the relationship reaching an endpoint.

THREE FACTORS THAT INCREASE THE PRESSURE NOT TO DIVORCE

Three significant factors highlight the pressure placed on a woman to remain in a marriage that has run its course:
- The assumption that a partner will change, which depends on the wife being forgiving and maintaining family harmony.
- If the couple has children, worries about their being distanced from their father and "losing their family."
- Religious beliefs about the impossibility of dissolving a marriage.

Let's look at these three reasons in more depth:

Reason #1

Family and friends might advise a wife that her husband will change and any mistakes should be forgiven because it is better to keep the family together no matter what. Alternatively, they may suggest that the husband's mistakes are not too bad, and maybe the wife provoked the negative behavior, so *she* should consider changing. This line of thinking is indicative of patriarchal ideology, which holds that a man's faults or missteps are a response to a woman's behavior. For example, cheating is justified if his wife is *"not good enough."* If he has a gambling or drinking problem, it is because she *"doesn't support or understand him,"* and he needs a way to cope with this.

The pressure on the wife is two-pronged. First, she should forgive her husband for the sake of family unity, *trusting that he is going to change.* Second, she should forgive him because his actions might be a consequence of *her failure to understand and be a positive influence for him.*

After more than twenty-five years in practice, seeing women in situations like this, again and again, I believe it is unlikely that a husband who is unfaithful, abusive, or dealing with substance abuse will change. There are exceptions, of course, but *once a pattern is set, it is hard to break free.* Women deserve better than to endure this type of harmful relationship.

Reason #2

Mothers who are thinking about divorce must also consider the well-being of their children. How will a separation or divorce affect the children and parent-child relationships, especially if the children perceive the divorce as the "mother's decision?" What about if one parent moves out of the house and the children no longer interact with him or her on a daily basis? What about external perceptions that children in divorced families come from "broken homes"?

In reality, a mother seeking a divorce is not going to destroy her family. Usually, by the time a woman considers separation, her marriage has likely been under stress for some time, and the children have picked up on the tension and problems their parents are experiencing. *The family has been severely affected already.* However, this does not make the circumstances and questions any easier to deal with.

Reason #3

In particular religious and conservative contexts, marriage is forever—a union ordained by God and sacred in the eyes of the faith—so it is impossible for people to end a marriage. Fulfilling one's responsibility to family is part of God's highest will, and supersedes personal happiness and fulfillment. In these traditional environments, a marriage ends only when death parts the couple.

THE COMPLICATIONS OF CONSIDERING DIVORCE

Getting a divorce is distressing—even if it happens under the very best of circumstances, it is still *a significant life change*. We are choosing to separate from the person we committed to love, the person with whom we have gone through good and bad times, the person we have given so much of ourselves and our time to, the person we have relied on for comfort and support. But then, if in the midst of considering such a difficult decision, the people we love and respect—such as family members, elders, and religious or community leaders—advise us not to divorce, *the situation becomes more complicated and painful.*

Family, friends, and others are usually legitimately trying to help, but they may not know all the elements of the couple's situation. Because of feelings of shame and guilt, or the pain of talking about difficult issues, the woman may not be able to communicate the full gravity of the situation. She may be embarrassed. Perhaps she is still processing the matter and is not yet clear on her thoughts and feelings. So people who offer even welcome advice might be *acting on incomplete information*. In some cases, people who pressure others not to divorce might genuinely *believe that divorce is wrong*. Their help comes from a place that is authentic to them, but that does not necessarily mean *it is in the woman's best interests.*

Putting these factors together, we can see how powerful the pressure not to divorce can be. Women under this pressure sometimes decide to divorce anyway but often with much guilt about their decision. Other women continue to struggle through their marriage, gradually experiencing more problems and suffering due to their untenable situation.

Debbie, a mother in her forties, shared her story: "It's been years since I've felt happy in my marriage. My husband has a gambling addiction. But for so long, I never told anyone how bad it was because I truly believed he would change. That didn't happen. Instead, his habits got worse, and life became more complicated as debts stacked up. I didn't have enough money to manage the household, and I had to lie to our friends about our availability to participate in social activities. I told my sister I was contemplating divorce, and she reacted very negatively: *'How could you do that to your children and the family?'* Her reaction made me reconsider staying in my marriage. But things are getting worse. My husband has become abusive, not only psychologically but also physically. I don't know what's worse, the physical abuse that leaves me with bruises, or the emotional abuse that tears at my self-esteem. I started wondering if this situation was my fault. I've prayed for a change, but what I received is more mistreatment. What can I do? *Where did I go wrong?*"

PRESSURE COOKER

The pressure to marry plus the pressure not to divorce

Another factor that complicates the pressure not to divorce is the initial pressure to get married. Particularly in conservative environments, women face many demands to marry and become mothers as part of fulfilling a woman's "natural destiny." Seeking a divorce means *putting an end to this "natural" and respected situation*, which goes against societal expectations. For a woman, trying to reconcile these factors in her personal life can be very difficult, especially if she has internalized these social pressures.

THE FEAR OF STARTING AGAIN AFTER DIVORCE

For those of us who have been married or in a long-term relationship, our identity becomes linked with that of our spouse or partner. Our existence is closely intertwined with this person's life; we share days and nights, families, hobbies, social circles, and more. If being part of a two-person entity changes—even when it is something you want—it is new and sometimes scary to step back into the world as just yourself, in a single-person identity. *We may find it difficult to make decisions, or we worry about being alone or whether we want (or would be able to find) another partner.* We may have to deal with new economic factors, especially if our partner provided us with a comfort zone of financial security and stability. *The future feels uncertain, and that creates worry and fear.*

REFLECTIONS: TAKE RESPONSIBILITY FOR YOUR LIFE AND HAPPINESS

Marriage works when it provides fulfillment and well-being for the partners as individuals and the family as a whole. This requires love, respect, consideration, and care from both parties. *Obligation alone* cannot make for a healthy, happy marriage over the long-term.

If you are in an unhappy marriage but feel pressure not to divorce, consider these points:

- Getting a divorce is difficult, is hard work, and profoundly affects everybody involved. However, staying in a lousy marriage can also be painful and create barriers to feeling hopeful, happy, and fulfilled in life.
- Social support is invaluable during any stage of life, but especially when you are experiencing difficult circumstances or making a change. Know whom you can go to for understanding and help, whether practical or emotional.
- Consulting a professional may be beneficial for support in evaluating your relationship. For instance: Is there a risk of harm? Has the situation deteriorated beyond repair? Is it possible to make positive changes with time and counseling? Are both parties committed to developing mutual understanding and communication? Do the partners feel love or attraction for each other? Are any other parties influencing on the relationship?
- If there's any risk of abuse, seek outside help as soon as possible. Once a pattern of domestic violence starts, it usually escalates.

Whatever decision you make, be sure you have the resources and support you need to follow through. *Permit yourself to ignore societal pressures in order to do what is best for you.* You are responsible for your life and happiness, and you owe yourself a fighting chance.

8

The Pressure to Be a 'Good Woman'

Sharon had been up since the crack of dawn cleaning the house and pressing her husband's work shirt. She prepared her children's breakfast; got them up, fed, dressed, and off to school; and kissed her husband goodbye as she handed him a packed lunch. Then it was time to bake pies and clean the house before heading to the school bake sale. Next, she attended a meeting of the church committee she co-chaired, which planned recreational events for the seniors' home.

She had to get home before her children so she could supervise their homework and cook dinner. Usually, she would have attended the evening prayer meeting, but she was not sure what time her husband would be home. After feeding the children and tucking them in, she walked the dog, responded to a long email from her mother, and called a friend going through a difficult personal situation. Sharon finally went to bed after emptying the dishwasher, exhausted but pleased to have made it through another day doing all that was expected of her as a "good woman."

If you understand Sharon's nonstop activity, you may relate to the heavy pressures and exhaustion that come with the expectation to be a "good woman." Women from conservative backgrounds, ethnic minorities, and religious communities, where traditional gender roles and expectations for women are strong, are particular targets for this pressure.

Another aspect of the pressure to be a good woman is feeling that your family and community expect you to make the same life choices as your mother, grandmother, and other women in your family. If you are not happy about that and want to try something new that better suits your interests and goals, others may interpret this as "selfishness." It is precisely *the opposite of the self-sacrificial nature a good woman is supposed to display.*

WHAT IS A 'GOOD WOMAN'?

In this chapter, I use the term "good woman" to describe the type of woman who strives to meet *the ideals and expectations for women according to a patriarchal worldview.* The good woman assumes a place subordinate to her husband (or other men in the family). Her husband is considered superior, the head of the household. She is a wife and mother (or working toward this ultimate goal) and committed to family above all. She cooks, cleans, and takes care of the children and household because this is the "perfect" role for women—and housework is beneath a man. If she is single, her obligations are to her parents and the rest of her family, including younger relatives and any family members with special needs.

The good woman is modest, restrained, and discreet. She puts the needs of her family and community first. She places herself, her wants, and her wishes last—in fact, she may not even think of her interests at all. She pleases her husband in all ways and makes him look better without drawing attention to herself. She is active in her community and children's school. She is a devout woman who does good works. She is virtuous and resilient, prepared to defend her lifestyle and choices to anyone who asks. She, in turn, is a role model to other women. In the workplace, the good woman's role is a subordinate one; it is assumed that she would not be interested in, or capable of, taking on a leadership role.

In traditional communities, people's personal and social lives are especially interconnected, with plenty of gossip about other people's private lives. So maintaining the *right image* is critical to success and a sense of belonging. If a woman does not act the way a good woman does, she may be perceived as a "bad woman," which can cause considerable *stress and fear about her future.*

If a woman resists conforming to society's expectations of a good woman, she may be labeled as "weird," "unconventional," or "odd." She may find her usual social circles less welcoming. Moreover, she may be misunderstood, *which can leave her feeling unsure about what she wants or whether it is worthwhile to follow her dreams.*

CHARACTERISTICS OF A GOOD WOMAN

Some of the behaviors and attitudes associated with being a good woman seem fine when we think about them in a vacuum. For example, sometimes you do have to put others' needs first; also being kind and doing good for others can be rewarding.

What is important to consider is the *context.* We must question even good actions if they are the result of an *oppressive system that creates intense, rigid expectations and harmful pressure in women's lives.* We should ask: *Who benefits from this? Whose voice is heard or not heard?*

Here are some further characteristics of a good woman:

Self-denial

A good woman puts herself last in order to put others' wishes first and ensure their needs are met. She is taught it is selfish to be independent, to think of herself. She turns down no request; the answer is always yes.

An offshoot of this line of thought is that being a wife and a mother, with all the self-sacrifice and caregiving this entails, is the best role for a woman. A woman could not ask for more and nothing could make her happier than to be a wife and mother.

Capable and busy

A good woman is a skilled homemaker, excellent parent, and very, very busy doing everything she can for her family, church, and community. She is never idle. At home, she is the first to rise and the last to go to bed. She participates in church and community gatherings, festivals, dinners—serving and attending to everyone without taking a moment for herself.

People-pleaser

A good woman is friendly and pleasant to all, agreeable, a people-pleaser. She intuits the needs of others and responds even before the request is made, serving with efficiency. This behavior is related to being subordinate—always saying yes, not voicing her opinions, and making others happy. The good woman often bites her tongue so as not to provoke others; she does not get angry or think ill of others; her emotions are "positive."

As the expectation to please others usually derives from loved ones or respected elders, there is no room for questions or refusal. That expectation is linked to the idea a woman must do and say all the right things to find a suitable husband or the right social circle.

Submissive to her husband

The good woman is married, and the husband is the dominant person in the family and household. The man provides for the family and makes the decisions because he is considered to have the necessary competence and experience. The wife supports him and defers to him for better or worse. *She must be happy with what he offers and not ask for more.* By being submissive and letting her husband lead, the good woman ensures her partner's appreciation and the safety and security he provides in return for her knowing her place. As she has attained her destiny as a wife or mother, she is expected to be satisfied and so has little right to express disapproval regardless of what her husband does or doesn't do.

Because the man of the house has the last word, *what goes on between a husband and his wife is only the couple's business.* Even if abuse occurs, in general, others have no right to intervene. As a result, domestic violence is prevalent in traditional communities, but people outside the marriage may not know the couple is having problems. In an environment where the relationship is closed from external view and input, the woman, as the "lesser" person, not only is often the target of the abuse but also is frequently blamed for marital difficulties or the husband's problematic behavior. It is assumed that either the woman played a part in the problem developing or that she is responsible for resolving the trouble and helping her husband change.

In addition to the risk of experiencing abuse, women who are repeatedly blamed and shamed are more likely to experience a decrease in their well-being, and to develop depression and anxiety. [22]

Virtuous

Because of the stereotype that women are pure and kind by nature, the good woman is responsible for *upholding virtue and goodness* in the household, whether in managing her husband or raising the children. Taking responsibility for others' misdeeds is part of a good woman's self-sacrificial nature, and crediting others for her good deeds or skills is "humility." If something goes wrong, if the husband or child makes a decision with negative consequences, the woman will be blamed for not foreseeing the problem; not providing enough love, care, or understanding; or not working hard enough to fix things—that is, not living up to the expectation of being "good."

Unambitious

A good woman does not have the experience her husband does since her life revolves around the home and caregiving. She also should not be as intelligent as her husband or a potential future partner. A "real" man will not want a relationship with a woman who is as smart as or smarter than he, so *she should hide or undervalue her capabilities and dreams*. In this environment, it is considered unfeminine for a woman to have clarity about her wishes or to be ambitious or aggressive in pursuing personal goals.

Focused on family and caregiving

A good woman is a mother (or working toward becoming one). This is considered the "highest calling" of a woman's life. As raising children and managing a household will take all her time and energy, she should not even think about having a career. You have probably heard of a "family man." However, it is likely you have never heard the term "family woman" because the expectation is that a woman's focus is her nuclear family.

A good woman is also expected to be the primary caregiver for her aging parents, in-laws, and any family members with special needs. It is the daughters, never the sons, who get tasked with these caregiving roles. With all these obligations, there is no time to think about personal desires and aspirations!

This environment is stressful for the good woman but is perceived as the height of all that is possible for women. Consequently, *women in this situation find it difficult to make changes in their lives.*

This was Diane's experience: "It takes so much effort to make my marriage work and make my family happy that I've stopped struggling to change things. I have to live with the fact that I'm just a housewife and a mother. Trying to do anything outside of these roles is a problem, and I don't want more difficulties. I feel like I'm going in the opposite direction of most women these days, but the easiest thing for me is not to rock the boat. *I never thought I'd get stuck by being a good woman.*"

Grace had a similar story: "I've struggled for years with being a housewife. It's not that I want to be wealthy or famous, but having nothing to do besides cook and clean at home is exhausting. I did choose this life. It seemed exciting at first to feel like a 'real' woman. I wanted to be home with my kids and take care of my family, go to church on Sunday, and do whatever I could do for our community. But it's been a few years, and I want more than being a housewife.

"Our home has been my little kingdom, but our kids are growing up, and soon they'll leave. My husband and I are in a routine of being together. This life is all I've known, and I don't feel confident to go beyond what I'm familiar with. I think other people look down on my being 'just' a housewife. *But this all started with the pressure I felt from family and friends to be a good woman.*"

All the components of this ecosystem act in harmony, and changing something may jeopardize a good woman's status—a significant risk. Being a good woman is about doing precisely what others expect, and since her primary role is to respond to those obligations, why would she need to change anyway? Her life is hectic, but she is *respected and recognized* for what she does.

THE PITFALLS OF THE "GOOD WOMAN" IDENTITY

Adhering to the ideal and pressure of being a good woman provides a type of status for women. By accepting this identity, they can find fulfillment, success, a sense of self-realization, and recognition from others. However, this identity revolves around being a wife, mother, homemaker, and caregiver, and has roots in patriarchal concepts that portray any interest or involvement in matters outside the family and home as secondary.

Because the good woman identity is connected to the roles of wife and mother, achieving this identity requires the woman to display the characteristics listed earlier to be attractive to the type of man who will make her a good woman. In this way, *the good woman's identity comes from her relationship to a man, not from her capabilities and potential.* She does not need to develop her character or pursue possibilities other than those that enable her to think, act, and live in a way that meets others' approval. If she shows dependency, submissiveness, and modesty in her relationship with her spouse and family, she gains a social comfort zone that rewards her for being "good"—attentive and submissive to the wishes of others—even if it comes at the risk of diminishing her power.

REFLECTIONS:
SHAPE YOUR LIFE YOUR WAY

A good woman is taught from a young age that if she is kind to others, she will be respected, accepted, appreciated, and treated well. *This simplistic belief ignores the complexity of human nature and the reality of human interactions.* No matter how nice we are, we cannot control the behavior of others. People will act and react based on *their nature* and *the moment,* not according to how good and pleasant we are. Other people's actions are their responsibility.

As human beings, we have an essential need for love and belonging, and the pressure to be a good woman can be so intense that a woman denies her essential nature and needs.

I encourage you *to be confident in your right to explore and pursue your inner desires.* No personal voyage is easy, however. If you are a young woman making your way, you may find that your social circle does not agree or approve it, perhaps to the point of excluding you from people and places you love and respect. Although this is painful, be confident that, however your journey develops, one outcome will be *learning about yourself and all that you are capable of doing.*

Your identity and destiny are unique to you, and *you are free to shape and form your life* without conceding to the expectations and pressures of others. *Take possession of what is yours, and do the best you can!*

9

The Pressure to Be Heterosexual

Frances shared her story about coming out to her parents when she was a young woman:

"I realized I was lesbian when I was thirteen. I had feelings for other girls, and I liked to be close to some of them who were okay with this. As I got older, my parents were kind of surprised that I didn't want to go out with boys. When I was sixteen, my best friend told me she loved me, and we started dating. It was hard to come out to my parents, but I finally said something one day. My mother began to cry, and my father didn't say anything. I went to my room in tears.

"My mother eventually came to my room and said they would help me become 'normal.' She asked me not to talk to anybody about this 'problem.' I remembered a friend who had come out to her family, and they took it very hard; they thought it would ruin their standing in the community. I also remembered a movie we saw where people were in hell for being homosexual. My mom said that I was *just young and confused*, that one of these days I was going to meet my dream man, and we would forget this ever happened.

"My dad, who was usually so warm, became sharp and withdrawn toward me. I felt terrible and confused: Why did I feel the way I did? Why did my parents react this way? How would my friends or our church act in response to my coming out? What would my future look like not having a 'normal' life? *Is being gay a punishment for something I did?* I thought that being attracted to other girls was immoral, shameful, and my fault in some way, that I must have done something wrong.

"At school and church, I started avoiding the people I felt would judge me. I spent a lot of time at home and lost some of my friends. My father was distant with me; I felt that it was difficult for him to tolerate my presence. My mom went deeper and deeper into depression. I was very alone and had many negative thoughts about myself and my 'problem.' I was distressed about how it affected my parents. I started having insomnia and other health problems. *I felt like my life was not worth living.*"

Heterosexist attitudes are prevalent across cultures and religions, many of which criticize and condemn homosexuality. Heterosexism assumes that everyone is heterosexual (attracted to people of the other sex)—that this is what is "right." Any other sexual orientations are seen as "unnatural," "deviant," "wrong," and "inferior."

If you have stood up to this pressure and are moving forward in life true to who you are, *you are demonstrating great strength and resilience.*

WHAT IS HETEROSEXISM?

Heterosexism is a system that favors heterosexuals and heterosexuality as the dominant sexuality. This system is prejudicial and discriminatory toward those who have homosexual or bisexual sexual orientations.[23]

Society has internalized heterosexism as a norm. For women, this standard translates into an expectation of being in a heterosexual relationship, marrying a man, and having his children. When something becomes a norm, it turns out to be society's standard for what is right and proper. Individuals who cannot or do not comply with the dominant pattern become the minority and subject to prejudice.

At a broader societal and structural level, most traditional religions believe homosexuality to be "sinful." They speak against and shun people of other sexual orientations. We can also see evidence of heterosexism by looking at how laws, services, and benefits are structured. For instance, laws and civil services (housing opportunities, employment laws, benefits) that favor traditional male and female marriages and relationships and do not give equal rights to people or partners of other sexual orientations are an example of institutionalized heterosexism and discrimination.

People are expected to comply with the norm or risk facing censure—not only at a societal level but also closer to home, at the family level. Communities and families might reject an individual of a different sexual orientation, believing this to be wrong and inappropriate. When it comes to something as personal as sexual orientation and its place in our identity development, it is *difficult and painful to be questioned, judged, misunderstood, and possibly even rejected*, especially when a person is young. So the pressure from society to comply with heterosexist norms is intertwined with our natural desire to be loved and accepted by our family and friends.

As a result, some young women may hide or deny their sexual preference and try to have heterosexual relationships that follow traditional feminine roles. They may also have legitimate concerns about their physical and psychological safety if they were to challenge heterosexism.[24] For these reasons, homosexual and bisexual women often opt to appear in social and work environments as though they are adhering to normative gender roles.

A woman who does not perform according to society's sexual identity norms is considered a sexual minority woman (SMW). A heterosexist perspective may consider her not a "real" woman because she is not attracted to men. Further, SMWs may be thought of as mentally unwell—in fact, homosexuality was considered a psychological disorder by the American Psychiatric Association until 1973.[25] Some people still believe homosexuality is a mental illness that can be treated—that LGBTQ+ people can be "cured" and become heterosexual.[26]

WHAT ARE THE CHARACTERISTICS OF HETEROSEXISM FOR WOMEN?

For women, the discriminatory pressures of heterosexism and sexism are often combined. Sexism is based on patriarchal ideas that emphasize traditional gender roles—men given superior value, women considered inferior—and cultural views on the limited roles available to women in order to be accepted.

In most societies, women are expected to perform the specific femininity that is valued by their culture. In sexist environments, power, prestige, and opportunity are concentrated in men's hands; women may be able to access some of these resources if they are feminine, attractive, and submissive enough to the men in their society. Supreme importance is placed on a woman having a relationship with a man for her to have a place in society, love, sexual pleasure, and security.

Sexism and heterosexism establish norms for interactions and relationships between women and men as well as for individual behaviors. Both support keeping the balance of power in men's hands (patriarchy). Because the man is considered superior and the head of the household, traditional marriage roles between a man and woman serve to keep women in check. If a woman behaves outside of sexist norms (for example, a feminist), some aspect of the social order is altered, and she may not be liked or accepted. If a woman lives outside of heterosexist norms (for instance, a lesbian), she turns society-expected norms on their head.

SMWs may experience, first, the pressure of sexism because they may not meet society's expectations for performing femininity and may be associated with negative stereotypes of feminists (for example, aggressive, hostile, self-centered, unlikeable individuals). Secondly, they face the pressure of heterosexism with all the prejudice and discrimination commonly directed toward people who identify as LGBTQ+.[27]

For an SMW, in addition to not being feminine enough, she is also not attracted to the "highest-caliber person" in her society (the alpha male), so *she doubly breaks the expected social pattern of how things should be.* You may have heard comments about lesbian or bisexual women not knowing the "real love" or "real pleasure" that comes "only" from having a sexual relationship with a man, or "missing out" on the comfortable life a man can provide for the woman who pleases him.

Although society is changing, moving toward providing equal acceptance and recognition of LGBTQ+ rights, in many countries homosexuality and same-sex marriage are still illegal.[28] Often there is *total silence about female homosexuality*; it is not even considered a possibility for a woman. Consequently, SMWs may have no safe space to talk about or explore their sexual identity and be under extreme pressure to stay in the closet.

The inability to be open and authentic about who we are can lead to *psychological distress.* Many SMWs develop *hypervigilance*—heightened awareness that can increase their sensitivity and emotional reactivity to the behaviors of those around them. Being in this state of constant stress for long periods can harm one's health and well-being. It takes great strength and resilience for SMWs to stand up to the pressure to be heterosexual.[29]

"I was sixteen when I started dating a female classmate, and I thought I had to come out. My mother was suspicious about my behavior, that I'd never had a boyfriend and didn't care about girly things. I was very good at math, science, and sports, and my mom sometimes said that competing with boys made me unattractive to them. I was afraid of rejection if I came out because I knew my parents expected that within a few years, I'd start dating seriously, get married, and have a family.

"When I did come out, my mother looked at me as if she couldn't believe what I was saying. My father asked *what kind of life I'd have without a husband to take care of me, and a family of my own.* He said that life and love with another woman would pale in comparison to having a man in my life. I know he said this because he thought it was in my best interests. But I told them I didn't care because everyone is different, and *we don't have to follow what society expects of us blindly.* I'm attracted to women, and I don't want to hide it anymore."—*Dorothy*

INTERNALIZED HETEROSEXISM

"I've always been attracted to women for as long as I can remember. I thought it was wrong, so I felt ashamed. I blamed myself for having these thoughts and feelings, but *it's the way I am, and there was nothing I could change or do except to keep this part of myself secret.*

"I knew my parents and family expected me to get married. My older sister was already married, so I was next, but I didn't want to. So in addition to being ashamed of myself, I felt guilty that I didn't want to do what was considered right and proper. I didn't know what to do. *I felt such terrible isolation and guilt for just being myself.*

"I met Heather, and we became friends, then best friends. I was very comfortable with her, and one day I revealed my secret: that I'm attracted to women. She was the first person I ever told. She didn't say much but asked me not to talk about it. Little by little, I noticed she was communicating less with me and had a lot of reasons why she didn't have time to meet up and do things together. This was painful, and I realized that I was attracted to Heather. I didn't tell her about my feelings, but it made her indifference and the distance she put between us hurt more. Our friendship slowly finished, and I've been lonely. I feel ashamed that who I am pushed her away, and I worry that something like this will happen again. It makes me feel that *being true to who I am might not be worth the risk.*"—*Caroline*

"Sometimes I felt uncomfortable around other women but didn't know why until I met Melissa. I tried to avoid her at first, but she stayed in touch and dropped a big truth bomb on me: *I was avoiding women to whom I was sexually attracted*. I started to understand my life and experiences better. I was attracted to women, but since I knew it was 'wrong,' I couldn't even acknowledge to myself how I felt. *I did my best to silence and deny this part of me*. I'd tried to meet men, but as soon as they expressed some interest, I'd run away. I was always introverted, but I'd become more isolated and shy before meeting Melissa. I know my parents were concerned and wanted me to find a husband as my friends had. But that's not my path. Melissa and I got closer, and eventually we became a couple. My family doesn't approve, and I've had to make the difficult choice of distancing myself from them."—*Laura*

One of the reasons Caroline and Laura found their situations so problematic was that they *had internalized their culture's negative views about homosexuality*. Through internalization, an SMW takes on society's negative beliefs and attitudes about sexual minorities and develops an inherent dislike and discontent for her sexual orientation and herself. This can result in constant inner struggle and turmoil for the SMW between who she is and who she feels pressured to be. She may feel shame, guilt, resentment, unworthiness, even anger and hate, which affect her sense of self and inner strength.

Guilt is related to the feeling she has done something wrong, for which she will experience consequences. Shame may be a more deeply seated feeling when the SMW believes that who she is, is wrong and that her social circle and community will disparage her.[30]

PSYCHOLOGICAL DISTRESS

The responses and coping mechanisms an SMW uses to deal with societal censure and personal guilt/shame can create psychological distress that also leads to problems in interactions with family, friends, and coworkers.

These difficulties can range from isolation and disconnection to a complete severance of ties and relationships. Relational changes might be spurred by a desire to avoid the pain and discomfort of rejection, questioning, and discrimination. Nonetheless, the SMW still suffers from the loss of social support and potential future resources.

Psychological distress can manifest in other ways that affect the SMW's intimate relationships. The development of overdependence, breakup anxiety, extreme insecurity, need for constant validation, suspicion and jealousy, domestic partner violence, and mutual aggression are the most common problems. Some SMWs may begin abusing alcohol or other substances as a way to cope, which is likely to exacerbate an already challenging situation further.[31]

There are also consequences in social situations. Negative interpersonal reactivity is when a person responds to stressful social circumstances—for example, being bullied, excluded, or ignored—with depression, noncooperation, or anger. With time, the SMW may respond either by becoming more reactive or more isolated, which is associated with decreased social well-being, especially in bisexuals and young adults.[32]

IS HETEROSEXISM COMMON?

Heterosexism is still prevalent in many traditional, conservative, and religious contexts, usually in a fairly blatant manner. It is less evident in more liberal environments, and people may deny it exists because of the development of LGBTQ+ rights. However, heterosexism is still present—in *subtle but yet powerful ways*—whether in individual contexts (*"Maybe you like women because you don't think a man would be interested in you"*) or in systems (for instance, adoption agencies that do not allow same-sex couples to adopt).

CONTEXTS WHERE HETEROSEXISM IS ESPECIALLY PREVALENT

Rural areas

Heterosexism is widespread in rural areas where residents mainly adhere to traditional gender roles and consequently are unlikely to accept anybody who identifies as lesbian, bisexual, or transgender.[33] They are also not likely to have had much interaction with people who identify as LGBTQ+ because gay people in the community may feel uncomfortable being open about their sexual orientation.

SMWs who live in this environment may deny their true self and become invisible to avoid rejection. This reduces their opportunities for social connection and support. They may not know any another SMW who could provide them with positive peer support and guidance in becoming comfortable with their identity.

Religious communities

Most of the world's major religions do not approve of homosexuality or gay marriage.[34] Traditional religious leaders and communities believe that marriage is between a man and a woman, so same-sex relationships are actively opposed. Religious norms are changing, however. Some churches and faith practices have begun to modify their views and definitions of marriage.

Working class and low levels of education

One way to reduce discrimination is through education.[35,36] People with less education are more likely to perceive gender identity in traditional ways and have biases against same-sex relationships.

Older generations

Older generations have typically supported traditional gender roles and opposed same-sex relationships.[36,37] This is based on the conservative mores with which older generations were raised: that the institution of marriage should be between a man and a woman and is primarily for the purpose of forming a family. However, a shift is beginning toward increased approval of same-sex marriage.[37]

REFLECTIONS: THE IMPORTANCE OF BEING YOUR AUTHENTIC SELF

Who we are attracted to is an essential part of who we are. To be lesbian or bisexual is *an identity*, not a behavior. *There is nothing as fundamental to human beings as identity*—it is the backbone of who we are; it is how we define ourselves. Our identity gives meaning, support, and strength to our daily life and personal story.

If you are an SMW and have faced heterosexism, you may have been questioned along the lines of, *"Why have a relationship that gives you fewer possibilities, less positive recognition, less pleasure, and more problems?"* This line of questioning is indicative of a denial of gay identity, as though an SMW could manage her orientation by making more "convenient" decisions. It does not take into account that *your sexual identity is part of who you are and that accepting it is the foundation of respecting yourself.* Moreover, you would not be able to change this part of you even if you tried.

If you are heterosexual, think about how you would feel if someone pressured you to be attracted to, and pursue a relationship with, a same-sex person:

- *What would your initial reaction be?*
- *How would you respond to this pressure?*
- *What does this pressure make you feel about who you are and your identity?*
- *Is this pressure helpful to your well-being?*
- *Do you think it is right that others pressure you?*

Working through this exercise may give heterosexual people an idea of the *damage heterosexist pressures can cause.* We are all responsible to end heterosexist discrimination, which hurts so many and limits people's opportunities to live a healthy, happy life.

If you are a sexual minority woman, *keep living your life in a way that is true to your identity and that helps you strive for new possibilities, build resilience, and experience happiness.* Remember it is not right to isolate yourself. It is crucial to find like-minded friends, safe spaces, and a sense of community so you can benefit from the support and guidance of others, who can lift you up.

10

The Pressure to 'Have It All'

Carrie told me her story when she came to me for assistance:

"As far back as I can remember, there were many things I was supposed to do in my life when I grew up. I was going to find *Mr. Right* if I stayed pretty and thin. I was going to study something leading to a good career, like science, engineering, or medicine—while also creating space to raise a beautiful family. I was going to be the best version of myself.

"When I started college, I spent a lot of energy trying to figure out how to accomplish these objectives. I knew there were opportunities ahead, but I didn't know how to reach them, and I blamed myself. I thought I was worthless and insignificant. I didn't know what to do to be happy and content in my life. And I was afraid to stop doing the things that my family said would make me 'who I was supposed to be.'

"What made these low moments even harder was thinking about the expectations my family had for me and the ones I had for myself. I ended up distancing myself from my parents and sister and shut down socially. I had repeated thoughts about not being good enough or assertive enough to go after my dreams. *I want to focus on the reality of what's possible instead of feeling ashamed because I can't figure out how to have it all.*"

The pressure to "have it all" is intense and overwhelming, *leaving many of us feeling tense, conflicted, and exhausted.*[38] This pressure has roots in both patriarchal stereotypes of women and second-wave feminism. *The contradictory messages and clashing ideologies underlining this pressure make it challenging to live up to.*

From the patriarchal point of view, the pressure on women to have it all means being *a good woman*—becoming a wife, mother, and caretaker who puts others' needs and dreams before her own.

From the other side, feminism urges women to pursue success in all the areas men have done because women are equally capable. Women are encouraged to be independent, have a career, put themselves first, accept no compromises, and pursue all possible options and outcomes for their life.

The combined takeaway for women is that they can *have it all* provided they *do it all* and *do it all well*. For instance:

- Be an expert in your field of work and stop at nothing in growing your career.
- Form and maintain a great family life with a partner who loves and supports you, respecting your independence and goals.
- Raise your children with access to every possible opportunity (extracurricular activities) to ensure a good future for them; supervise their homework and liaise with their school.
- Keep up with household chores: cooking, cleaning, gardening, and more.
- Pay close attention to and invest in appearance—face, body, hair, clothing, and accessories.
- Make time for exercise (maintain and improve physical appearance) and self-care (be present, focused, and relaxed); carve out time for yourself.
- Have a vibrant social life personally, professionally, and as a family. This means always be ready to accept invitations or invite

people over (keep the house impeccable at all times); have the perfect outfits for you, your husband, and your children for every situation; be energetic, engaging, and a great host (never tired or wishing for a moment of peace for yourself).

- Let everyone know how great having it all is via social media. Post about amazing family times; beautiful, do-it-yourself parties; and relaxing vacations.
- Do all this with grace, wit, poise, and charm!

The reality is that most women make a remarkable effort to have it all. We multitask and juggle a thousand routines but wind up feeling depleted because of *the prevailing idea we can always do more or do better.* Feelings of shame and guilt hover over us, ready to pounce, due to the excessive demands of our own and others' expectations. There is no regard for the practical realities of women's lives, the potential for stress and burnout, not to mention the availability of time and resources.

The freedom to do it all *sounds* great. Instead, we are often in conflict between the positives of new opportunities and the negatives from trying to do and have it all at once—and to show others that we did it.

WHY IS THIS PRESSURE SO DIFFICULT?

As I said, the pressure to have it all is based on contradictory patriarchal and feminist premises that lead to *conflicting messages* about how women should organize their lives and set their priorities. This conflict is what makes the pressure to have it all so excruciating.

Others may have divergent expectations for us. Problems arise when we do not respond to these conflicting expectations equally, or if we meet more some than others based on our relationships rather than the nature of the expectation. For instance, if a father expects his daughter to be a professional, she is likely to try to live up to this, even if she has other interests, because of the importance of her father in her life.

When it comes to social expectations, everybody feels the press of some kind of *obligation*, because expectations are related to ideals of how things should be. If a woman does not act according to expectations, she may feel shame about how others see and judge her actions. People can feel shame and guilt simultaneously, leaving them feeling remorseful, judged, embarrassed, and humiliated.

Doing it all does not necessarily result in having it all, which can lead to frustration, shame, and guilt. We may feel we are coming up short but cannot figure out what to do differently to accomplish more. We may also be worried that other people will recognize we do not have it all and think there is something wrong with us.

PRESSURE COOKER

The pressure to have it all is linked with the pressure to be perfect, the notion that women have to do it all correctly from the get-go, without mistakes or imperfections. Expectations of instant perfection inhibit creativity. There is no room for trial and error, exploration, growth, and discoveries along the way to the desired outcome. We also internalize this expectation of perfection; if we cannot do it all or have it all—and flawlessly—we are inadequate, and we feel ashamed about this. The twin pressures of perfection and having it all are severe: *they contribute to stress and unhappiness, and rob us of inner peace and balance.*

HOUSE OF CARDS

The pressure to have it all can become all-encompassing. It is like a house of cards. If one card is removed, the entire structure weakens or collapses. If all aspects of a woman's life are going well, but she and her husband are having a rough patch in their relationship, others around her may devalue all her other accomplishments and skills. This is quickly personalized: *there is something wrong with her (me); she (I) did not try enough; she is (I am) not capable.* Here are other examples of how this can play out:

Emma's career is going great, her marriage is outstanding, her children are excelling in school, but Emma is a little overweight, which becomes, *"She must not be very disciplined."*

Janice is an outstanding mom and housewife and does not have a career outside the home, which becomes, *"I'm failing in being a role model for my daughters, and I don't help my husband because I don't contribute to the family finances."*

Karen's career keeps her busy, so she can't always attend her children's school and sporting events, which becomes, *"How could you be so selfish and have your priorities this mixed up to put your career before your family?"*

Under pressure to have it all, a woman is a success in all areas or she is a failure; there is no middle ground. She is either *valued and appreciated or criticized and belittled.* Being confronted with these false either/or absolutes affects our self-worth and self-esteem. This is serious because healthy self-esteem is vital to motivation—the driving force of our lives.

KEEPING UP APPEARANCES

Social media can add to this pressure, as it allows us to pick and choose images or messages that give others the impression all is perfect in our world. This can provide us with momentary gratification, as others like or comment positively on our posts. Nevertheless, trying to maintain this positive feedback can lead to stress and comparing, whether within ourselves ("Is this as good as that was?") or with others as we try to "keep up with the Wilsons." We may also feel we cannot be honest about the struggles and awkward moments we face as part of life.

"To other people, I'm someone who seems to have it all: I'm a good lawyer. I have a wonderful husband and two kids. I stay in shape. In real life, I keep my worries and concerns hidden from others. Nobody wants to hear that you are worried your kids are becoming addicted to video games, or that you and your husband have barely any time to spend together, or that you didn't get the promotion you wanted and feel like a failure. If I shared those worries with someone, I'd either hear about how I can do better or that I should think about all the good things I have and be more grateful. To avoid that, the 'face' I put on is that I'm happy, satisfied, and confident—*and the charade of 'having it all' goes on!*"—*Elizabeth*

"From what everyone can see of my social media and public appearances, I have it all and am very 'happy' because I'm an actress. My life seems glamorous, and everyone assumes that things are perfect and all my dreams are coming true. *The truth is I'm always tired physically and mentally.* I constantly worry about the future and the high stakes of failing. When will the next job offer come? Will someone else who's more beautiful or talented get that great role? I'm struggling on the inside. But I show people the opposite. I'm afraid to share my deepest concerns."—*Nancy*

REFLECTIONS: FIND YOUR OWN PATH AND TIMETABLE

If trying to have it all leaves you feeling exhausted, stressed, or confused, *consider other approaches that can work better for you.* Pursue your goals and dreams in your personal and professional life, but do so according to your path and timetable rather than based on societal pressures. We have to develop resistance to this pressure.

Determine what the truly fundamental elements of your life are right now, what your essential goals are, and *start from there.* Know you can develop your interests over time. You do not have to do everything or have everything at the same stage of life. *You can start with one of the choices you have prioritized for now and plan for the future development of other possibilities.* Along the way, you can prepare for these future routes through reading, studying, and networking.

It is also helpful to look at your *concept of success* and whether you might need to redefine it, so "success" is not measured by responding to social expectations or external achievement. Think about what personal satisfaction means to you. Can you connect it more with character growth or developing personal confidence?

Enrich your well-being by cultivating *self-respect* for who you are, what you want, where you can go, and what you can be.

11

The Pressure to Remain Silent When Exposed to Sexual Harassment

Julie got her first job as office manager assistant when she was a college student. She was both new to the workforce and inexperienced in interacting with men, so she was unsure of the appropriate boundaries in this new environment. Julie's boss took an interest in her that quickly crossed the line into embraces, touches, and sexual comments that made Julie uncomfortable. She thought *maybe she was the cause of his behavior and blamed herself.* Was it something about her clothes? Was her skirt too short or were her pants too tight?

Julie said, "I struggled in this environment, but I needed the job to pay for college. And it was in an industry related to my field of study, so it was good for my resume." However, Julie's boss's advances increased over time, and she became afraid to be alone with him. *"I was scared he would assault me,"* Julie told me.

Eventually, she decided to quit. She told no one why or about what had happened. "When I read about the Me Too movement, I realized I was a victim of sexual harassment," Julie said. "That recognition and validation from others with a similar experience *freed me of the nega-*

tive thoughts and feelings I had about myself. I know how deeply painful sexual harassment can be, and never again will I remain silent."

Sexual harassment or fear of it happening can create a lot of pressure and stress, especially for women in the workplace.[39] If you have had a negative experience like Julie's, you also know *the shame or fear of retaliation victims feel about coming forward with their story.*

WHAT IS SEXUAL HARASSMENT?

Sexual harassment is inappropriate, unwelcome behavior of sexual nature that negatively affects or threatens someone's economic or job security, employment, or promotions opportunities.[40] It often occurs within an *unequal power dynamic.* The most common form of sexual harassment is when a man in a position of power takes sexual advantage of a less powerful woman, who risks losing her job or advancing her career if she rejects him. This behavior can go unchecked with no consequences for the perpetrator but *shame, blame, and fear of retaliation on the part of the victim.*

Sexual harassment has a long history, but the specific term came into being in the 1970s and has since received increased awareness.[41] For many decades, sexual harassment occurred under *a veil of silence in both private and public environments.*

In the workplace, it was considered an unpleasant circumstance but *par for the course for women,* who had little recourse to defend themselves or prevent unwelcome sexual behavior without risking their employment. What followed was the assumption that a woman with a successful career owed it to sexual favors and the backing of the man (or men) who had taken an interest in her—not her skills and hard work. If a woman did not advance in her employment, it was because she did not understand the "unspoken rules" of the workplace or "play the game." *The dichotomy and clash between "good" and "bad" women were re-created in the workplace.*

WOMEN DISPROPORTIONATELY EXPERIENCE SEXUAL HARASSMENT

Sexual harassment is still widespread in work settings where power is a factor in determining relationships between people. Both women and men may experience sexual harassment, but women are targeted more frequently. U.S. studies found "that anywhere from 25 percent to 85 percent of women report having experienced sexual harassment in the workplace."[42]

The reality is that businesses are still less likely to promote women to senior management roles,[43] so men are more commonly in positions of power and therefore more likely to take advantage of power dynamics to hire, promote, or fire women, including in unscrupulous ways. Women who are less assertive and ambitious (part of the socialization of women to be "nice") may be easy targets for harassers.

When a woman is sexually harassed within an imbalanced power environment, it is not uncommon for her *to stay silent and not take action, fearing repercussions.* She may be worried about retaliatory measures, such as losing promotion opportunities or even her job, and being criticized and blamed for what happened. Also, importantly, because of her silence the woman receives little to no social support, which negatively affects her well-being.

BLAMING AND SHAMING THE VICTIM

Blaming the victim is a common tactic to keep people silent about sexual harassment. Harassers (and, frequently, others in society) will say their inappropriate behavior was incited by how the woman dressed, walked, or talked. Some might suggest the woman is trying to "take a good man down" and ruin his reputation. The survivor *risks not only retaliation in the workplace but also being shamed and blamed into silence and viewed with contempt in the community.*

Sexual harassment is a humiliating experience that can affect someone on many levels, as Sophie's story shows: "I worked in retail for many years, where the guiding principle is that the customer is always right. But this was taken to an extreme in my workplace: I had to smile and respond politely even when customers made disgusting or taunting comments or tried to grope me. I didn't say anything because I was afraid my coworkers might think I was exaggerating, and my boss could dismiss me without notice. My boss and job security were on one side, the customer was on the other side, and I was the middle, the one who would take the blame if anything went wrong. With time, I started thinking that the inappropriate touching and comments were my fault, something I provoked. *I felt a lot of anxiety about going to work but also terrified of not having a job.*"

When it comes to sexual harassment, women have to consider their safety, well-being, and self-respect as well as their professional standing and opportunities. Being a team player in some companies may come with the implicit understanding that employees *do not "complain" about each other.* If reporting sexual harassment is seen as "complaining," women risk their jobs by coming forward. And if they do end up telling someone later when there is less risk of ruining their careers, there are fewer chances offenders will be punished due to the passage of time. Women who do report harassment run the risk of being accused of *misinterpreting "normal" interactions or a sense of humor, being "sensitive," trying to gain personal or economic advantage, or ruin a man's career.*

Women might opt not to report for any number of reasons: feelings of degradation and humiliation, fear of retaliation, embarrassment, being blamed for the harassment, or interference with their careers. While we can encourage women to let their voice be heard, at the same time, sexual harassment victims should not be pressured to report harassment officially or unofficially. They should be informed regarding their rights and supported in acting according to what they feel is in their best interest.

MEN AND AWARENESS OF SEXUAL HARASSMENT

Unfortunately, many men are not conscious of the very real problems of sexual and gender-based harassment. This may stem from their specific *contextual learning and socialization*, such as if women are objectified or viewed as inferior in the man's culture, or if the man is from a *generation where traditional gender roles and expectations of male dominance were the norms.*

In general, because patriarchal ideology gives men power and entitlement, it blinds them to how harmful sexual harassment is. They may not grasp the importance and cross-society benefits of gender equity. Men have an essential role to play in changing the culture because they are still more likely to be in positions of power and leadership.

Another reason some men do not fully understand the problem of sexual harassment is that they perceive their interactions with women as a *courtship game*, in which the man keeps trying, the woman keeps refusing, the man continues until the woman gives in, and the man achieves victory. The more the woman rebuffs his advances and declines invitations, the more this signals to the man that she wants him, so the more he is attracted to and pursues her. Of course, *a woman may decline because the man's pursuit makes her uncomfortable.*

However, the man may not realize his behavior is offensive or disturbing to the woman

REFLECTIONS: SEXUAL HARASSMENT IS NOT YOUR FAULT

If you have been harassed, *do not blame yourself.* Harassment is not your fault or due to your actions or "mistakes." There will be people in your workplace and community who support you, believe you, stand up for your career, and help you move beyond this negative experience. If you feel comfortable speaking up, your voice will help shine a light on this critical issue, support positive change, and help others know they are not alone.

If you witness sexual harassment, you can support the victim by believing her, helping her feel safe and comfortable, standing up for her and what is right, and supporting her decision to report the harassment or not.

When sexual harassment goes unchecked, we all suffer for the simple reason that *power is being used destructively.* We are each responsible for standing up for what is right and being positive role models in our circles of influence. We are all worthy of working and interacting with others in a safe, respectful environment, where we can contribute our skills and develop our potential.

We need to be present, focused, and working toward genuine solutions to this problem. *When our workplaces are healthy, safe environments, everybody wins.*

12

The Pressure Not to Opt Out of Your Career

Nicole, one of my acquaintances, confided in me about the pressure she was facing as she considered being a full-time, stay-at-home mom. "Even my parents are giving me a hard time about it," she said. "*Nicole, you're just getting your career off the ground. How could you give up now?*" Her colleagues had been surprised too: "*You're so smart; I don't understand why you're considering this.*" Nicole was suffering from stress and doubts about making a bad decision.

As you may have experienced in your own life, women often feel obligated to have a career or climb the corporate ladder because the messaging we hear is that these *are the best avenues for women to be empowered personally and economically.* To choose being a wife and mother over a career is often seen as an inferior choice or a non-feminist decision—a throwback to the 1950s housewife.

There are many negative stereotypes about women who do not pursue a career path; for instance, that they are lazy, taking advantage of their spouse, or have diminished lives. Of course, women decide to opt out of a career for a vast number of reasons, but many approach this decision as a *real vocation*, and we should respect this.

I have spoken with many women as they considered how to manage their careers alongside starting or raising a family. Many worried they would be seen as boring, unsuccessful, or taking the "easier path" if they chose to be a stay-at-home parent, or if they made their career a secondary priority by choosing less ambitious roles or part-time work. Some felt shame and guilt, like they were failing others or themselves by not pursuing their career. They wondered if they would come to regret not exploring their "full potential."

While most of the pressures I discuss in this book are informed and driven by patriarchal ideology and paternalistic concepts, the pressure on women to have an upwardly mobile career in order to be perceived as successful perhaps derives more from a second-wave feminist perspective (albeit this, too, is in response to patriarchal structures).[44] The second-wave feminism of the 1960s and 1970s included a focus on how familial and marital societal norms of the time and previous generations affected women's equity in society and the workplace, and contributed to the wage gap.[45]

For generations, success has been measured in power and assets—salary levels, career positions, and achievements—and this was the domain of men who had the opportunity to develop a career (usually with the support of their wife), while women's place was in the home. In the '60s and '70s, the pendulum began swinging away from the notion that women had a single, inescapable destiny: to be wives, mothers, housekeepers, and deferential to the men in their lives. Instead, women were encouraged not to "settle" for matrimony and family life because women, too, could have it all.[46]

As the turn of the millennium approached, the contemporary feminist view developed: *rather than elevate one choice over another, women have the freedom and right to choose from any number of options and to pursue what gives them real satisfaction.*[47] There is no single definition or path to being a successful woman, and women can personalize their path in life and the way they achieve their goals.

Here is more of Nicole's story in her own words: "I'm an engineer by training and used to work for a prestigious company. It was a challenging, interesting role, with great possibilities. I was also in a relationship that became the most important part of my life. My partner is from another country and getting married to consolidate our relationship and start a family was important to him. I come from a family where most of the marriages were affected negatively by careers, leading to quite a few divorces. I also wanted to live together and start a family, so I quit my job to move and get married. My coworkers, especially the women, couldn't believe my decision—they said I had so many opportunities ahead of me. *I knew that I could choose any path, and the one I wanted was to get married and start a family.* My husband and I agreed that when we had children, I would stay home to care for them; we felt it would be the best for our family."

Nicole's choice is unconventional in that she made a decision that her peers and family did not expect in this day and age. The critical difference, and what sets Nicole's story apart from the experiences of women in the early to mid-20th century, is that it was Nicole's choice—*a choice she made free from external pressures.* For Nicole, being successful and happy meant prioritizing family life over a career path.

CONSIDERING THE PROS AND CONS

Stepping away from a career for family reasons—whether it is a full- or part-time change, or a switch to a less ambitious path—is a big decision for a woman and her family. There are several things a woman may want to consider, including the economic viability of the decision—both for the family as a whole and for herself in particular, as she will be economically dependent on her partner. This can be a significant change, not only financially but also psychologically, especially for someone used to feeling in control of her income and resources.

Maria and Mark married after a long relationship that started in college. When Maria got pregnant, they discussed their plans for the future and decided she would quit her job before the delivery. They had a good relationship and made the decision together, but it still hit Maria pretty hard when she left her job. "I thought of myself as an independent woman, and suddenly I was going to be financially dependent on my partner," Maria said. "My friends didn't agree with my decision; they encouraged me to rethink it. To be honest, there were times when I wasn't sure about our plan. *I felt like I was moving against the flow of women's progress.*"

Mark also began feeling increased stress at work. As the family's sole earner, he began to worry about making enough money and the possibility of being laid off. Both of them felt their relationship wobble under the weight of their worries about finances and the guilt Maria felt about having to rely on her husband as the breadwinner. "What helped us," she said, "is that we kept communicating with each other, and we decided to change our perspective concerning our family."

Maria and Mark started thinking about adapting their lives to their possibilities. They adjusted their lifestyle expectations and switched to activities that required less spending, such as cooking at home instead of going to restaurants, hiking, and gardening. They made new friends who shared their lifestyle goals. Maria felt a lot of satisfaction in parenting her children hands-on and investing in quality time with them. "We have two kids now, and looking back on the last fourteen years, this has been the happiest time in our lives."

Maria and Mark's story brings out the value of partners communicating about family financial decisions and staying flexible and creative in making lifestyle adjustments, evaluating the decision as new factors arise. For women considering being the stay-at-home partner, it is also important to weigh up the possible repercussions of these decisions, financially as well as concerning personal goals, feelings of self-worth, and relationship dynamics. Depending on a partner to be the wage earner can create perceptions of inequality in the relationship that affect the stay-at-home partner's confidence about her resource contributions and level of say.

Raising a young family is a significant time in a parent's life that comes with a lot of hard work and opportunities for growth in all areas of life. Parenting skills are transferable assets mothers can take with them, whether they stay at home, return to the workplace, or branch out in other ways.

REDEFINING SUCCESS

Being "successful" has commonly been measured in terms of money and power. However, more and more, people the world over are *redefining what success means to them*. Some choose a high-powered career, others a less intensive job that gives them freedom and time over a six-figure salary. People may raise a family or opt out of starting a family. They are looking at personal markers of fulfillment, self-realization, individual and family objectives, meaning, and inner peace.

Women's markers for personal success are not limited to pursuing an ambitious career path, achieving power, or making money. *Women's freedom to control their lives means each one can individually define what being "successful" is for her and take pride in following that road.* Some women will consider many possibilities, including career paths, or choosing to be a stay-at-home mom and homemaker as a vocation. This is their decision and merits appreciation.

Jennifer's story is an example of this: "I got married at twenty-six. We lived in another city far from our parents, and when we had our first child, we didn't have any family nearby to ask for childcare help. It was difficult for us to think about putting our little one in daycare full-time, so we decided I was going to quit my job. I was pretty sure it was the right decision, but I wondered every now and then because of the time and money I'd already invested in my education and career. My family and friends were also concerned. Everyone said I needed to keep my career options open to have a successful life, but the reality is that there's no cookie-cutter way for women to be successful nowadays. Success may be career-driven for some women, but for me right now, *it's making my family flourish.*"

REFLECTIONS: DECIDING WHAT YOU WANT AT ANY STAGE OF LIFE

We are all different. We have different backgrounds, preferences, and experiences, so we make different choices. It is shortsighted to think there are only one or two successful choices or paths for all women.

Women are not limited to choosing between having a career or having a family. *At every stage of life, we can redefine what success looks like for us and what we want to achieve.* Freedom is making our informed decisions. There is new growth to be gained in forging our authentic path rather than responding to the expectations of others.

We can decide what we want at any stage of our life. We can make creative decisions to move ahead and live on our terms. Everything is open for exploration—and this is invaluable! *Take pride in choosing the options you feel will bring you achievement, delight, and fulfillment.* Take pride in living out your choices. That is the key to real success.

PART 2

WOMEN IN CONTEXT

In part one of this book, I presented the different social pressures women experience. In this section, I will address a variety of real-life situational or personal contexts women may find themselves in—circumstances that may or may not be of their choosing—and the issues relevant to consider in those scenarios.

This approach is helpful for women in situations they didn't opt for who want to learn more; women who desire to enter a particular context; and women who want to get out of, or change, their current one. This information might also be beneficial for parents, partners, friends, teachers, counselors, and advisors who want to understand and help women in any of these conditions.

Comprehending our context is essential, not only because it includes our present—where we live and work, our experiences and interactions with family and friends—but also for how it can influence our future and potential. Our context is informed by our culture, which affects our attitudes and approaches to life issues, related social pressures, and the opportunities available to us.

In this section, I will explain the pros and cons of various contexts. I will talk about the possibilities and limitations of these environments and how women might approach challenges or evolve within them. I will share my reflections on how women can find more joy, meaning, and fulfillment in these contexts.

I will describe various *"personas."* I use this term to explain how a woman in a specific context may experience, inhabit, or portray different characters, personalities, or faces depending upon the circumstances she is in and the moment she is living. The *persona* is a way in which a woman understands herself and presents herself to others, whether consciously or subconsciously, as she moves through various points and experiences in her life. The personas in the chapters are not displayed in order of importance or chronology, and it is essential to note that a woman may even experience more than one of these personas simultaneously.

Two points crucial to understanding personas are *circumstances* and *moment*. Circumstances are how we are situated in relation to internal or external; and favorable, unfavorable, or neutral conditions. The power of the present moment is what predisposes us to act or not, to look inside or outside, and to evaluate our resources in a particular way. *Who and where we are at a given time has a significant bearing on how we feel, think, and act.*

13

Single Women

I n many environments, marriage or its equivalent—having a stable, long-term relationship—is still considered a woman's primary goal and most significant accomplishment. A woman's dream and destiny should be to get married, have a family, and raise children. Everything else is secondary to this core aspiration.

Exposure to these gendered expectations begins at a young age. Girls are encouraged to play with toys that reference this cultural pressure, such as dolls, kitchen sets, and model houses. Of course, many things have changed in recent decades, and expectations for women have expanded. It is common for them to pursue education and a career, and to wait on marriage until their late twenties or into their thirties. However, *many of these women experience concern and fear at the prospect of "being alone" beyond these ages.*

As I already mentioned, single women typically receive a lot of pressure from family and friends to start a relationship. *Being single is a problem that needs a solution*, and a woman's family often expects her to draw attention to this matter, believing this problem will get worse with time and become impossible to solve. In conservative or religious environments, there are also clear family expectations for a woman who remains single: she becomes the caregiver of aging parents or other family members with health or care needs.

The following are examples of situations single women may find themselves in and the *"personas"* they may experience or display as they move through different circumstances and moments in their lives.

Circumstantial

This woman is single due to circumstances—for example, she has ended a relationship or is divorced, separated, or widowed—rather than direct choice. Particularly in the case of a spouse's death, the circumstantial single woman finds herself in a situation she did not choose. Also, in any of the above cases, she may see it difficult to return to the lifestyle and conditions she had before the relationship. Neither she nor her circumstances are the same.

Feelings of loss and grief may compound her experience of being alone plus memories of her former partner and their life together. If she is now a single parent or co-parenting with an ex-spouse, this adds further challenges. She may want to find another partner later in life or prefer to stay single. Either way, however, her circumstances are not entirely of her own making.

With time and positive support, the circumstantial single woman may adapt well to her new situation and enjoy the new experiences and challenges it brings her. She can discover unique aspects of herself and expand beyond her comfort zone.

"After my marriage of twenty-five years ended, I didn't know what to do; I couldn't remember how I was back when I was single. I wanted to be in a long-term, committed relationship again, so I joined an online dating service, but nobody I met or dated was interested in something long-term. I started to feel somewhat down until I realized that *being single was an opportunity to focus on things I wanted to do for myself.*

"For example, I wanted to improve my career prospects, so I took some classes at a local college to upgrade my skills. As a result, I got a promotion and salary raise. I used these funds to spruce up my apartment. Then I began traveling with friends—that was unbelievable! Many beautiful things are happening because of this big life change and also because *I've adjusted my perspective. There are so many possibilities ahead.* It's my life, and I'm free to decide what to do without having to worry about others' expectations!"—*Helen*

Concerned

This single woman has not yet found "the one," but *feels under pressure to do so.* She worries that her biological clock is ticking down, and she would like to have a stable partner before getting pregnant becomes a problem. This stress or pressure can *backfire*: the more emphasis she puts on herself in the search, the fewer opportunities she seems to find.

The concerned single woman is very much impacted by social pressures to find an acceptable partner, which makes her search a difficult one. It is often when we relax and let go that we see what we are looking for. She is often afraid of *making the wrong choice or being more invested in the relationship than her partner.*

"A couple of months ago, I met a guy at the gym. We started texting and decided to go on a date. We had a great time talking and found we had a lot of common interests. I was excited to get to know him better. However, after a few dates, he became more distant and slowly stopped responding to texts. I said to myself, *it's happening again!* Even the guys I feel I have an excellent connection with end up walking away within a few weeks. *What am I doing wrong? Am I boring? Do I seem desperate for a relationship?* Or, is it something about the men I keep dating? It makes me confused and anxious. To top it off, my family is pressuring me about getting married. I'm going to be thirty-six next month. They say it's my fault I'm still single."—*Barbara*

Needy

The needy single woman struggles to form and maintain relationships. She has often been unhappy during her relations and feels profoundly disappointed and cynical about the possibility of being in a good partnership.

Women who have suffered abuse may experience this persona because the unhealthy relationships they have been in *significantly impacted their self-confidence and self-esteem*, and hurt their emotional growth. At the same time, they feel pressure to find a new partner or spouse, because *they are looking mainly for safety and belonging*. Unfortunately, their feelings of low self-worth make it challenging to find partners who will respect and treat them well, and they usually find themselves in a painful, vicious cycle of poor relationships and increased suffering.

"I was twenty-nine when I met Dan. I had recently gotten out of a relationship that ended badly because my ex was cheating on me and lying about it. In the beginning, Dan treated me like a queen. I liked that. I enjoyed being with him. *I don't do well being on my own.* Our relationship moved quickly, and soon we were living together. But not long after, he started being physically and psychologically abusive. He would get drunk and insult me, yelling that I was fat, ugly, stupid. My sister found out and advised me to leave. However, I couldn't, because *I didn't know how I could manage on my own—practically, but emotionally too.* He knew I wasn't going to leave and kept on abusing me. He used to say, 'Where the hell are you going to live?' He started cheating on me, staying nights out, until one day he moved out with another woman."—*Patricia*

Authentic

This woman has made a conscious decision that being single is interesting and gratifying to her at this time in her life. She enjoys her lifestyle, freedom, and having her own space. She usually has an exciting career, close friendships, interests, and hobbies. *She is comfortable with her single status, living alone, and resolving situations by herself.* She may have potential opportunities for starting a relationship, but it is not her primary objective. If a chance for a relationship arises, she considers it and makes her decision freely and autonomously.

Career-oriented

The career-oriented single woman has priorities different from the traditional ones: a career is more important to her than a romantic relationship. These women commonly have fulfilling but demanding jobs and may believe a personal relationship or raising a family will interfere with their projected goals. Many of them have meaningful, active social lives. They do not engage with traditional societal pressures and expectations for women and instead *develop their path, creativity, and dreams.*

"My family considers me an 'old maid,' and I don't care. I'm single, and that's how I've chosen to live my life. My job requires a lot of travel and networking, and I love it! My career gives me the opportunity to contribute to others in significant ways. *Of course, sometimes I feel lonely, but it's impossible to have it all.* I wouldn't be able to maintain my career and keep up with a partner and family at this point. *My life is what I want, and I'm grateful for it.*"—Jessica

CLOSING THOUGHTS

We cannot control all the variables and situations that might happen in life, but *we can choose to take advantage of and enjoy the opportunities that come our way.* If we are single, it might just be because we have not had the chance to establish a unique connection with another person. Alternatively, maybe we have explored this option but find we prefer solitude and personal space, or we need a particular, single-minded focus to accomplish our goals.

If you are a single woman, here are four points to consider:

- When you are single, you have an *ultimate say in your decision-making*, whether in your personal, social, or job life. You can choose to do what works for you and what you enjoy.
- When we shift our attention *to focus on what we have and can do*, we will experience more positive thoughts and feelings. For example, finding a partner involves many variables beyond your control. However, you can look at your interests, talents, and resources, and set related goals for yourself.
- Know that living alone does not necessarily mean living lonely. You can find and enjoy a social life and good company almost anywhere, including with family, friends, colleagues, and your greater community. Many people live alone these days and *appreciate their independence and freedom.*
- Be mindful that, whatever your situation is, you always have an opportunity *to contribute to others' well-being*, which can give

you great pleasure and fulfillment. Finding ways to give to those around you is an opportunity for personal growth, discovering new paths and possibilities, and developing creativity.

In this personal journey, you can connect with others who are in similar situations and share your positive attitude. Side by side, you can move forward, build, and grow. *Through being mindful of what you have and can do, and cultivating your progress, you will find your destiny.*

14

Childless Women

I n part one of this book, I discussed how women who choose not to have children are viewed with incredulity. *"How can you want that? How can you be so heartless and self-absorbed? You're going to regret this decision!"* On and on the comments go. You can understand why childless women may feel defensive when people comment on or ask judgmental questions about their choices.

In traditional environments especially, womanhood is equated with motherhood—there are no replacements or alternatives. A woman who does not want children is seen as not in agreement with her true essence as a person.

Many women do opt to become mothers, whether because it is what they want or they feel it is what family and society expect from them. In the latter case, these women may have decided on this path after serious consideration, or they may be too young to assess the pros and cons from a personal standpoint, or they feel too much pressure to do anything but follow the traditional path.

At the other end of the spectrum are the women who have decided that being a mother is not for them. They have other objectives and want to pursue a different journey in life. They may find satisfaction and fulfillment as a single woman or with a partner. However, some of these women still internalize society's reaction to not following the path of motherhood and may feel there is something wrong with them or with their relationship, as in Lisa's case:

"My husband and I met eleven years ago and started a relationship soon after. We got married after we had been together for a year. Suddenly, we felt a lot of pressure from family, friends, colleagues, and even neighbors, to think about having children. I feel like an outsider when I say that I don't want to be a mother. *It seems that I won't be able to sync with society on this.* I don't want a baby. I never did. *Is there something wrong with me?* My husband also doesn't want to have a baby— but his decision came after we talked about this. *Is there something wrong with our relationship?*"

Family and friends' unsolicited advice and opinions about having a child put much pressure on women or couples, even though this input is offered with good intentions. Many childless women and couples report feeling an immense burden related to other people questioning and judging their decision.

A childless woman in a happy relationship told me, "It almost feels like *the worst way to respond to the question of having children is to be honest and say, 'My partner and I don't want to have kids.'* Because then everyone feels compelled to tell us about how important and wonderful it is to have children and all the consequences we'll suffer if we don't."

MISCONCEPTIONS ABOUT VOLUNTARY CHILDLESSNESS

One of the misconceptions about women who choose to be childless is that their lives are incomplete, that they lack the excitement and fulfillment of raising a child. In reality, many childless women are content with their lives and ability to invest in their careers, interests, personal experiences, social life, and travels. Personal growth and contributing to others can come through many forms other than motherhood. Each of us is unique, and whether or not we are mothers, a *variety of choices and paths are available to us.*

Women who are voluntarily childless may have chosen to be so because of a particular lifestyle that requires independence and solitude, a career that requires single-minded focus, or because they do not want to be responsible for another person—or any number of other reasons, all of which are valid for these women and deserve respect.

In general, women who choose to be childless have thought about their decision, whether they would be a good parent, and especially whether they *want* to be a mother. Some have wished or tried to become a parent but eventually concluded this path would not work for them, so they looked toward other objectives and avenues of fulfillment in their lives.

"I wanted to *want* a baby, not just *have* a baby, but this didn't occur. What happened was that I was in a long-term relationship and got pregnant unexpectedly. I started thinking about how my body would change, and more importantly, how our time and little space would change. I didn't want the endless responsibilities that would come with having a child, and my boyfriend had no desire to be a father. One morning I started to bleed, and my pregnancy was over. We both experienced a lot of conflicting emotions when I miscarried, but in the end, we were relieved and thankful that we could continue the life we loved."—*Cynthia*

A widespread misperception is that if a woman does not have children, her life will lack meaning. In my conversations with women who decided to be childless, a lack of purpose or meaning in their lives was the least of their concerns, because they were pursuing their avenues for fulfillment and self-actualization.

There are infinite possibilities available for developing creativity as a positive resource, building resilience, and making decisions that give significance to our lives. Of course, people may feel they lack meaning in their lives at some time or another, but it is not necessarily connected to not being a parent.

Another prevalent notion is that, if you do not have children, you will suffer loneliness and isolation during your older years. Experiencing solitude during the later stages of life is a legitimate concern,[48] but it is not limited to women who do not have children. People who have raised children may lose contact with them for various reasons, which may be even more painful.

Whether or not you have children, what is relevant are what path, career, and vocation will bring the greatest happiness to your life. This is the million-dollar question, and no single answer will be right your whole life. Regardless of our place of origin or upbringing, there are many factors in life that we are going to encounter. Whether or not we have children, we'll come across many opportunities for contentment, challenge, and everything in between in our lives. Both women who are mothers and women who are childless can develop in creative ways, live their dreams, and contribute to something that is meaningful to them.

TRENDS IN CHILDLESSNESS

Around 15 percent of American women are childless.[49] A significant number of voluntarily childless ones are highly educated.[49] Their reasons for being childless vary: they don't want to have a child, they feel it is not economically possible, they are not sure their current partner is the right person to have a child with, or they had a difficult childhood and are afraid to repeat the experiences they had growing up. Some women are childless due to health reasons or health-related concerns, such as fertility issues or genetic risks.[49] Partners with fertility concerns often have tried for many years to have a child but reach a point where they begin to rethink their future and family goals, or they try other methods of becoming parents, such as adoption.[50] Other women are still undecided.

PERSONAL CHOICE

Over the last few decades, an increasing number of women have been able to choose whether they will have children, just as they decide among other options in their lives. There is now more respect for choices based on people's authentic personal preferences.

Women also have a higher number of options in how they choose to become mothers—for example, biologically, with assisted reproductive technology, or via adoption, fostering, or surrogacy.

We also can take the initiative or collaborate with others in ways that benefit children, like "mothers" in creative, spiritual, intellectual, or financial means. I have talked with many women in this position. Some of them were initially reluctant to choose a path that differed from society's expectations but eventually felt at peace in choosing childlessness. Thus, they continued to live their life and pursue their dreams. Being confident in the knowledge that you indeed have free, personal choice is the only way to move forward with authenticity and meaning in life.

Deciding whether to have children has a lot to do with where you are in life personally and the circumstances you are in. Becoming a parent changes your life, especially how you see yourself and your world. In my case, when I became a mother, instead of focusing on myself, I started putting my attention and efforts toward my daughter, and that changed me into the person I am today.

Any major life decision changes us, for the simple reason that we become oriented toward our new direction. Our thoughts, feelings, and actions align with our chosen objective, and we begin to meet and interact with people who are part of this new world. *Becoming a parent or deciding to be childless is no different.*

As self-determination and personal freedom have become more the norm, people feel more comfortable forming or not forming families *according to their own choice.* It is a good thing when we can make authentic life decisions without fear of judgment and can support others in doing the same.

"When I got married, my number one objective for many years was to get pregnant. Did I want a baby? I suppose so, although in hindsight, I think the main reason was that I thought the point of marriage was to build a family. After five years of trying, including going through all kinds of fertility treatments, we decided to stop. It was a difficult decision for us, and it took time to come to terms with it. You can't rush the process of adjusting your views and expectations when all your hopes and goals have been linked to having a child. *But peace comes after a while, and we've continued building a life we love.* Now we feel the opposite. We don't want to have children. We're happy and exploring interesting things in our careers as well as in our personal and social lives. I see both the stress and exhaustion, and also the joy and beautiful moments that mothers I know have. It works for them, but I don't want to take on that responsibility."—*Michelle*

CLOSING THOUGHTS

Motherhood is one of many options women have in life; it is no longer seen as a women's only or ultimate destiny. Of course, becoming a parent is a valuable consideration, but we have *the freedom to decide among a wide array of choices.* I encourage you to give your personal wishes precedence over following the expectations of others and trying to please them.

Be true to yourself and try to understand what you want for your life. Decisions about motherhood are personal and rest entirely with you. If you have a partner, the topic of becoming parents is something you will eventually discuss and decide together. Ultimately, it is still your choice.

Because there is often heavy social pressure on women to have children, know that it takes much courage to follow a different path. Being a mother brings a lot of work and change into your life, so be sure you want that transformation. If becoming a mother is not your genuine desire *go into the childless option with confidence and joy.*

15

Housewives and Stay-At-Home Moms

Deciding to be a housewife or stay-at-home mom (SAHM) takes a lot of courage, for several reasons.

1. It is a solitary road because women who make this choice often receive a great deal of criticism about the decision itself as well as how they undertake these roles. There is much stigma around women staying out of the workforce to take care of the home or their children. It is seen as devaluing women while elevating men, rather than the husband and wife contributing to the family in different ways.

Much of this criticism and judgment comes from other women, either those who are also housewives or SAHMs but have different ways of doing things, or career women who may consider the stay-at-home choice a sign of failure. How we judge others is often a reflection of our insecurities. Judging allows us to see ourselves as being in the right, a place from which we can evaluate others' different choices as wrong, misinformed, and so on. Social situations lend themselves to gossip, which can reinforce opinions. We have to think about building mutually supportive bonds and collaborating with other women in a similar situation. We need to give and accept help to create an empathetic climate.

2. If a previously financially independent woman becomes a housewife or SAHM, she turns out to be more dependent on her partner financially and, perhaps, socially. In contemporary society, a great deal of personal value is derived from being productive in the world of work. Being a homemaker or a SAHM can feel like a throwback to the past, when bearing and raising children was women's fundamental destiny. Yet, making these decisions now do not have to be linked with the negative conceptions of the past. Instead, we should respect that some women choose this path in accordance with their authentic desires.

In my opinion, women's lives today are more complicated but also more fulfilling and rewarding. Many women want to be housewives and raise their children. Being a mother is an incredible opportunity, and women have the right to embrace and live this experience fully. It doesn't mean they don't value career growth and parity with men. Equality has to be measured not by the money an individual brings home but by each's contribution to the totality of the life both partners share in and benefit from. Being a housewife or SAHM has to be seen as equivalent to a commitment to a job, both leading to positive, complementary results for the couple.

3. Women who choose to be housewives or SAHMs for a period may have questions about the future, specifically about whether they will be able to reenter the world of work. This is a legitimate concern as technology advances rapidly and workplace culture changes. Women may wonder if their competencies and career skills will still be relevant a few years down the line and whether they will be able to return to an equivalent position.

During the time women are SAHMs, they will continue to grow personally, and they also have opportunities to develop professionally. There may be learning opportunities designed for busy people (for example, online or evening classes) and volunteering or networking meet-ups that SAHMs can take advantage of, particularly once their children are older.

Whether we decide to be a housewife or SAHM or return to the workforce in the same or a new career capacity, the main thing is to be sure that we act according to freely made, self-aware choices. This is the surest path to living authentically and productively.

Kathleen had many dreams in her adolescence and young adulthood—dreams of writing, studying geology, and traveling. However, she put most of these dreams on the shelf when she married a military man who was assigned to different posts across the country, and the family had to relocate often. She raised four children, often feeling like a single parent, as her husband was deployed for long periods of time. Kathleen's life was full-time busy with driving the children to school, activities, and social events. She felt a growing distance from her husband since they spent less time together. As the children got older and became more independent, Kathleen felt lonely. She thought she did not have many career-related skills and that it was "too late" to reinvent herself and take a new path.

However, one day Kathleen realized *she had been telling herself a negative story*. Of course, she was still capable of learning and doing new things! So at forty-eight, she looked at her options and decided to enroll in the training she needed to become a real estate agent. She is now a successful real estate entrepreneur and educator. "I'm proud of the decisions I made," Kathleen said, "both to be a stay-at-home mom and invest in my children, and then to take on something new, and stay active and productive."

Margaret's experience comes from the other side of the spectrum: she was a concert pianist, and her entire world was focused on practicing and performing. When she was in her thirties, she started dating a lawyer. It was a casual relationship at first, given Margaret's performing and travel schedule. Gradually their connection became stronger and the relationship more structured. For the first time in Margaret's life, she started thinking about quitting her job to start a new life with a spouse and raise a family—which she ultimately did.

Margaret's love for music never faded; she kept playing and learning in the comfort of her home but enjoyed not having to travel and perform consistently. Some of her colleagues felt strongly about her quitting a successful career. But Margaret was happy. *She had made her decision based on her changing personal preferences*, and her husband was supportive of her choices. Margaret talks about the two chapters (so far) of her life—the professional and the personal—without any regret or disappointment.

PERSONAS OF HOUSEWIVES AND STAY-AT-HOME MOMS

A homemaker or SAHM may take on or present different personas depending on her circumstances, level of satisfaction or dissatisfaction with her reality, and what is going on in her life. Here are a few of the personas a housewife or SAHM might inhabit.

Committed

Women with a traditional background usually have a committed persona, which is their preference. They believe a woman's rightful place is the home, and her primary responsibilities are taking care of her husband and children. Everything else is secondary to this endeavor. Convinced that this is their ultimate responsibility, most of the time they feel motivated and accountable to accomplish whatever tasks and goals are related to their family obligations.

Naïve

This woman approaches the roles of a housewife or SAHM in a simple, innocent, or trusting way. She may be young or inexperienced, and being a housewife or SAHM sounds like the right thing to do. Women from immigrant backgrounds who are not familiar with the culture and language of their new home may also relate to this persona.

Unassertive

Women with this persona are often timid, hesitant to assert themselves or speak up. They likely have been raised in traditional environments where strength is concentrated in men. They rely on their husbands for all decisions; later, they may depend on their older sons. Their self-esteem and confidence are minimal and usually limited to what they can do within the four walls of their home.

It may be difficult or impossible for them to imagine an autonomous life. If they someday find themselves with more independence, they will try to find another relationship. Housewives or SAHMs in this situation may be at risk of abuse. They are unlikely to talk with others about their situation, including domestic violence, because they may feel they are causing the abuse and deserve it, or they are afraid of losing the relationship.

Victim

Women who are unhappy with their situation and feel trapped and frustrated often blame others: their parents, husband, or children. Because they see themselves as victims, they do not recognize their own choices and self-determination as a potential path to resolution and getting unstuck. They do not take any responsibility for their situation. Consequently, when things go wrong, it is others who need to change, not them. Even when women find themselves in circumstances not of their choosing, blaming others is a negative approach, and a victim mindset makes growth and changes difficult.

Idealistic

Women living this persona have committed to a set of principles that guides their lives. They are likely to act in reliable, constant, resolute ways since they are trying to be loyal to a paradigm they trust. They feel responsible for the happiness and progress of everybody under their care and believe that living up to this ideal will result in their well-being and fulfillment. Anything that does not fit within the framework of their values is considered a distraction or interruption.

Resigned

We see this persona in women who did not choose to be a housewife or SAHM but felt they had no other option due to cultural, economic, or other reasons. They accept their situation as "fate" and do not actively try to influence or change where they ended up.

Rebellious

Women with this persona would not have chosen to be a housewife or SAHM if they had had other options—they do not enjoy their role. They are nonconformist and determined so they look to the future with the hope of changing their life.

DECIDING TO BE A HOUSEWIFE OR SAHM

When a woman chooses to become a housewife or SAHM, she should do all she can to prepare for this new route in life. Even if a woman has freely decided to leave a job or stop pursuing other professional endeavors, it is still possible, over time, that she may grapple with low self-esteem or feel disempowered. She may internalize the pressures others put on her and question whether she is doing the right thing. Her social life may change to revolve mostly around spending time with other housewives and SAHMs, who may feel a sense of regret or displaced identity.

However, the housewife or SAHM path is also one that a woman can *infuse with personal creativity and productivity to make the journey her own.* The starting point is realizing that we are lucky to be able to decide with a partner how we will approach life as a family. As a housewife or SAHM, your personal needs and unique identity will inform your own choices and the distinct contribution you make to those around you.

How a housewife or SAHM organizes her time and resources is up to her. There may initially be fewer external demands and pressures on her schedule, and her social environment will change. She may spend time at home alone or with her children, and have social contact with other women whose lives and schedules also center on children and home life.

The focus of her activities will change, too. If a woman is on her way to motherhood, she may at first be entirely focused on caring for her body through pregnancy and postpartum, then shift her concentration to the needs of her child (or children) as they develop from newborn to toddler, and on to school and related activities. After a woman's first child is born, her focus on herself, career, or relationships shifts to include the new reality of parenting.

For homemakers without children, their time may be concentrated on personal endeavors—for example, completing studies, upgrading work skills, or contributing to community or church projects.

CHALLENGES AND DRAWBACKS TO THIS DECISION

A woman who chooses to be a stay-at-home wife or mother enters a new world with new possibilities for gratification. Still, she may find herself missing some things, such as the sense of self-fulfillment that comes from a career–especially if her work gave her purpose, which is vital to happiness. We share many roads with others—from our infancy with our parents and siblings to our adolescence with parents, peers, and teachers to our adulthood with partners, children, and peers. However, one road is exclusive to us as individuals: our career path. Of course, we do work with others in a job environment, but each step begins and ends with self-determination, which can provide genuine feelings of gratification and accomplishment.

Another challenge is that a housewife or SAHM may not feel equal to her partner, who is now the primary provider. This adjustment is especially tricky if the woman previously considered herself independent and self-sufficient. Her self-confidence may be affected. She may think she is less interesting or has less to contribute to adult conversations because she is no longer exposed to new ideas or conversational topics from the workplace or time spent with friends. She may also worry that her partner will be reticent to share things or that misunderstandings will arise because they are operating in different worlds.

From my conversations with women who became housewives or SAHMs without considering this decision in its full breadth and depth, here are some of the most common challenges I have seen them face:

- Slowly becoming less active, since there are fewer demands on their time
- Developing negative habits, such as self-medicating, alcohol or substance abuse that interferes with caring for their children or keeping up with daily functions
- Losing their self-esteem, believing their decision to stay home a sign of failure
- Gossiping about other women to boost their sense of rightness and security
- Deteriorating relationships with partners because of envy, jealousy, and lack of trust
- Fears about the future and insecurity about their capabilities

CLOSING THOUGHTS

The decision to become a housewife or SAHM is a huge one that will have repercussions for you and your family. *Take your time making this decision, and consider as many aspects as possible.* Talk it over with your partner, and seek out external advice and support. Think about the following:

If an essential part of your sense of self is linked to your career or unique talents, we live in a time with many opportunities to be self-employed or work from home and have a flexible schedule. Companies may specifically be looking to hire capable, motivated people who can work independently. Opting to stay at home for a period or while you have young children does not mean you need to forgo working or having a career permanently. If work informs your identity and self-esteem, do not give up on that. Look for timing and opportunities that are right for you to be involved in a career.

On the other hand, if your sense of achievement is related to making a home and investing in the family as a full-time focus, being a housewife and SAHM is probably the right choice for you. This is just as valid an option as having a career. When your decision is rooted in your authentic self, it is connected to your identity positively—that is what will *increase your self-esteem, self-realization, and give you satisfaction.*

What is important is that your decision is a choice you have made freely, taking all possibilities into consideration, and that you and your partner experience *equity* in your relationship.

16

Rural Women

Rural women are not a homogenous group. They come from different backgrounds, experience unique circumstances, and have access to varying economic resources. However, in general, women living in rural areas face significant challenges due to the often-conservative nature of rural life.

Patriarchal systems and traditional gender roles, the most significant factors in the oppression of women, combine to make rural women's lives difficult. There are high expectations and intense pressures for rural women to be "good women" - to get married, to have children, not to divorce even if they are in an unhealthy marriage, and to put themselves last. Adhering to known and established norms and not having access to, or rejecting, other positions or possibilities can leave rural women feeling they are stuck in a repetitive cycle with no opportunity to break away from the system and develop their potential.

OBSTACLES

Two factors make it difficult for rural women to identify the pressures that prevent them from pursuing a freer, more personally rewarding life: rural culture, and poverty.

Rural culture

In general, rural people tend to embrace more *traditional values* and struggle with integrating new lifestyles or worldviews. They tend to be conservative in that they respect and accept what is conventional and customary; they are wary of new ideas, including changing traditional, gender-related norms. There is little tolerance for views or behaviors that differ from the conventional roles expected of men and women. Maintaining family and community ties and following expectations are paramount.

Rural communities are multifaceted, interconnected systems of formal and informal social groups.[51] People depend on each other for their economic and personal survival, especially if they are family members or neighbors, and develop various skills and abilities that enable them to support each other through difficulties.[51,52] The bonds formed from this mutual give-and-take between community members often make it possible for the community as a whole to be self-sufficient, to establish deep trust in each other but also distrust to strangers.[52]

Families are often close-knit and work together, so they try to avoid conflicts or talking about interpersonal problems or personal feelings.[52,53] People are expected to be patient and endure their difficulties, putting their issues in God's hands. There is a strong belief in the concept of fate—that we are on a path we cannot change, so we should accept our fortunes or misfortunes with tolerance. For all these reasons, it is uncommon for rural residents to seek external support for personal problems, mental health, or other counseling needs.[52,53]

The rural lifestyle is fraught with difficulties and circumstances that are often beyond human control, and communities face these challenges resolutely, supported by their traditional values, faith in God, and religious resources.[54] Religiosity—Christianity specifically—is robust in many rural American communities.

In this environment, it is tough to stand up for alternative ideas or activities, since people are expected to comply with traditional values. The greater good of family and community is what is essential. A woman must think about her spouse, children, extended family, and community first. To think of herself is considered a kind of selfishness. In any case, after attending to everyone else's needs, a woman typically has little time left for her own goals. Besides, people rarely consider that *she may want to try something else*, and there are few or no role models to support her.

In summary, the characteristics of rural life include self-reliance, individualism, traditionalism, distrust of outsiders, religiosity, strong work ethic, emphasis on family and community, and resignation to fate.[55] Rural inhabitants share dense social networks, with social and cooperative ties often going back generations, and they are collaborative and interdependent, especially in crisis situations.[51,56]

The following story illustrates these characteristics:

Melanie is the eldest child in a rural family. She has two younger brothers, and the grandparents also live with the family. When Melanie told her parents she wanted to continue studying after high school, they said the best path for her was to get married, be a homemaker, and raise her children. However, when Melanie's older brother wanted to go to college, there were many family conversations about this and short trips to visit a nearby college. Nobody talked about Melanie's potential to further her education. She, as the only daughter, would also have to be available as a caregiver to her parents when they grew older.

When Melanie said she would like to get a job, her parents said she could help keep the books for the family farm. Melanie had just turned nineteen when her mother passed away. She quickly assumed her mom's responsibilities, taking care of the house, cooking, and looking after her brothers. It was a hard time for Melanie: she felt the whole world was on her shoulders and that she had to give up her hopes for the future. She had no time to start, much less maintain, a relationship that would lead to marriage, and she had already let go of her past dreams of studying and having a career.

She started feeling lonely and depressed. Her days were filled with chores and making small decisions related to the household, but she felt no joy. Her brothers were becoming more independent and busy with their own lives. Melanie felt left behind with her worries and loneliness. Still on the surface, Melanie pretended everything was fine.

One day, during a family gathering, Melanie finally expressed how unhappy she felt. Her father and brothers said she should be comforted by the fact that she was able to fulfill the role of a good woman in the household. *This gave her some comfort, along with her prayers and talking with the town priest. She believes everyone has a destiny he or she must accept.*

Poverty

Poverty is prevalent in many rural areas. Combined with other socio-economic problems, it creates a vicious cycle that makes it difficult for rural residents to access education or employment opportunities that could lead to a better quality of life. As population movement continues to flow from rural to urban settings, living and working in rural communities has become more challenging, and these communities are shrinking or drying up altogether in many areas.[57]

Rural environments are especially unfavorable to women, given their multiple obligations (raising a family, caregiving, joining the family business), limited opportunities for education and employment, and traditional values that direct women to consider themselves last.

Young women are expected to subordinate their personal or career-related wishes, prioritizing family and community.[58] The absence of clear motivation and structure in rural women's lives[59] can contribute to early pregnancies, high rates of stress, and depression.

CHALLENGES RURAL WOMEN FACE

Overextended roles

There is a cultural expectation in conservative environments that women should consider the needs of others before their own, be the family caregiver, and forgo an independent career to prioritize home life. Given the importance of family and community ties, these expectations are especially pronounced for rural women.[60,61] They are expected to care not only for their nuclear family but also for elders, in-laws, other children in the extended family, and any family members with special needs. "Good women" should follow this caregiving model, putting themselves last, or risk being judged as "selfish."

The family caregiver role is not limited to mothers. It also applies to girls and young women. Older sisters are expected to take care of younger siblings and help with homework and cooking. Daughters are supposed to care for older parents in their later years. Older women take care of family members with disabilities or facing other challenges; they care for their grandchildren whose mothers are young, unmarried, incarcerated, or substance abusers.[62] Complying with these family and caregiving expectations takes many hours of women's time and keeps them tied to specific locations—their house or hometown. *All these pressures limit women's freedom, time, and flexibility to invest in other opportunities and personal growth.*

Violence against women

In rural settings, incidents of violence against women, especially domestic partner violence, are generally underreported for the reason that "what happens at home, stays at home."[63] A value system that teaches women to "grin and bear it" encourages *tolerance of domestic violence.*

Cultural factors linked with patriarchal ideology and the conservatism that is predominant in rural areas can contribute to the idea that *a woman is to blame for any abuse she experiences.* If a woman does not act according to expectations, and abuse occurs, the violence may be considered justified: the woman "deserved" the abuse because *she is not acting the way a "good woman" should.*

Another factor complicating spousal abuse in rural areas is that women don't have many opportunities to get help or leave the abusive situation. They may not know people outside the community, have the means to live by themselves, or may think their partner will eventually change. Even if women can overcome these difficulties, there are potential problems with reporting to the police, getting professional help, or being assured of confidentiality, which is crucial for personal safety.

Since rural residents are likely to hold conservative and religious beliefs, they are typically against divorce. Rural women may find their freedoms and rights restricted by patriarchal family structures and deep religious convictions. Since self-sufficiency is so highly valued, it may be hard to get help. Plus, conservative views commonly place the burden of resolving abusive situations on the victim—on the woman. Besides, women frequently blame themselves for the violence they suffer; they believe they are at fault and not worthy of help. They are afraid of being judged if they tell someone what is happening. *They feel alone and responsible for resolving a situation they fear they have provoked.*

Family and friends are typically supportive when nature causes a stressful event, but when it comes to interpersonal tensions and relational problems, they maintain distance. Domestic violence is considered a "family problem"—something *to be resolved by the couple behind closed doors.*[63,64]

Depression

Rural women may be at higher risk for depressive disorders.[65] Depression is particularly prevalent in women, especially if they face other risk factors.[66]

There is often stigma around mental health and suicide in rural communities,[67] which makes it difficult for women to express their struggles and receive assistance. Stigma is perpetuated in different ways. For example, if a rural woman dies by suicide, it may not be reported as such because of religious implications and to protect her family from harmful gossip. The community may be silently aware of what has happened, or even why; however, no one talks about it publicly.

IN SUMMARY

Social pressures in rural environments come from a particular combination of conservatism, patriarchal attitudes, adherence to traditional gender roles that elevate men over women, and limited availability of—and access to—social and health-related resources.

The multiple, significant pressures rural women face are linked not only to ideology and values but also to practical matters. Rural women are constrained to aspire to gender-stereotyped goals considered acceptable for women. Traditional gender roles indicate that women should be wives and mothers, taking a subordinate position to their husband, the head of the family. Women's primary purpose is to be caretakers for their children, household, and other family members needing assistance. Any work outside the home is likely to be a low-paying job or unpaid work in the family business.

Rural women's busy schedule of challenging responsibilities does not give them much time or opportunity to think about their own needs or desires. There is little to no exposure to role models who are stepping beyond traditional boundaries and pursuing their projects and goals.

If a woman does not respond according to the many expectations laid out for her, whether in her personal life, work, or activities, there are consequences, including the risk of abuse. Social environments that promote male dominance and disempower women are more likely to engage in and tolerate violence against women.[68]

"I grew up in a working-class family in a small town. I have an older sister and a younger brother. We have several aunts and uncles and a bunch of cousins. My mother didn't have a paying job—she believed it was the man's role to provide for the household. But she worked more than my father did, from early in the morning to late at night, seven days a week. I always felt she was treated unfairly because her work was noticed only when it wasn't done. The house was at all times clean and there was always food unless she was sick or visiting my grandma, who lived an hour away. My mother visited her once a week to clean her house, buy groceries, and stock her medicines. Still, before mother left, she always made sure things were in order and that we had a meal to warm up.

"I could see that my mother was always tired and concerned, never happy. However, she would look me in the eyes and say that what she wanted for me was to find a good man and have a family. *To dream of anything else was wrong, and our most important duty was to thank God for what we had.* Her only wish was to do more and do better.

"I got married shortly after my seventeenth birthday and had my daughter by eighteen. I was doing what my mom wanted for me. But I slowly learned that my husband was an alcoholic. When he lost his job, I had to figure out how to pay the bills. So now I'm a waitress in the local restaurant. I work long hours, and it's hard, but sometimes I make good tips. I hide most of the money, so my husband doesn't take it to buy gin."—*Amy*

CLOSING THOUGHTS

It is true that rural women often have to deal with a harsh, conservative culture. However, whatever your cultural background, and certainly if you are from a rural environment, keep in mind that *no single culture contains the full truth of what is right or how we should live our lives.* A culture presents certain viewpoints and a set of values for how to do things. But there are other cultural views and values we can learn from and add to our life.

On a personal level, your life—with all its originality and uniqueness—belongs to you. *It is your right to decide what you want to be and do.* Ground yourself in what is important to you, understand your present reality, and use whatever resources you can to keep growing. Be on the lookout for people and opportunities that can provide you with learning and support. Look for role models in your community, or make connections online to find people who can mentor and help you.

As you tap into your authentic self, you will be confronted by an enormous enemy: *your fears—fear of failure, fear of others' reactions and opinions.* People will respond according to their expectations for you, but you are not here to comply with the pressures others put on you.

You are changing so that you can live your life your way.

- Therefore, do not let fear of failure stop you. Of course, you will make some mistakes and experience disappointments, but you can use these as a springboard to grow and expand your creativity and possibilities.
- The golden rule for responding to fear is that if we confront—even in small steps—the situation that provokes it, fear becomes smaller and more manageable. It is when we do not look our fears in the face that they grow out of control and become unwieldy.

So stand up, trust yourself, look for helpers around you, and go forward in your life.

17

Religious Women

In this chapter, I use the term *religion* to refer to formal religion and religious ideology versus informal religiosity, quest religiosity, or spirituality. Formal religious doctrine often supports traditional beliefs regarding relationships between women and men, marriage, and families.

Most traditional religions of the world are patriarchal in nature. The man of the family has almost all the power; he is the decision-maker and can impose his wishes unopposed. Women are subordinate in this power dynamic, which also signals their obedience to their religion's leaders, teachings, and community. By submitting to their husband, they demonstrate that they are "good women," as is expected of them, and gain the related benefits of social acceptance and inclusion. The good woman is also a role model for the "right living" to her peers and younger women. *All these expectations pile up to create heavy pressures for women.* To top it off, these expectations are linked to "God's will."

Women in most traditional religions typically experience pressure to get married and raise a family. Religious parents and families expect and believe that young women should become wives and mothers who are obedient, submissive, and devoted to their husband and children forever, no matter what. It is crucial, especially from a religious perspective, that women carry out the role of a wife in respectful, modest ways. Many women believe that following their faith means pursuing this path, without considering other possibilities.

The following is the story of Rachel, a woman in her thirties who was going through a difficult situation related to these issues.

"Since I was young, my parents and grandparents talked about the beautiful future I would have when I meet my husband, the man who will love and protect me. They said that nothing would be more rewarding or make me happier than starting a family. That was the idea I grew up with, that one day I was going to meet *The Man, The One*, and that would be when real life started.

"I wasn't sure about the happiness part, though. I saw my parents argue, dad blaming mom, and mom crying. When I asked her what had happened, she'd say it was adult stuff and I didn't have to worry about it. I saw that she was resigned to the situation being what it was and endured those uncertain times patiently.

"My family's expectations for marriage put me under pressure. Instead of enjoying dates and relationships, I was looking for *The Man* who would change my life. I started dating Bob, who eventually became my husband. He had been a friend from school, devout and well-respected. Our first few months of marriage went pretty well, although I felt Bob was too controlling about my time with friends. He wanted me at home instead of going out. I was twenty-six, we didn't have children, and I thought what I was doing was entirely right. But he just became more controlling and rigid. I couldn't believe it!

"One day we argued, and Bob said we should talk over our differences with our religious leader. So we did. He listened to us, and after a moment, he said that *I* was wrong. That Bob had his reasons and was doing the appropriate things for our marriage. That I needed to see that Bob was right and become the good wife he deserved.

"I thought I was good, but I guess for our religion and Bob, *a good woman puts her wishes last to please her husband, family, and the religious community first.* I can't do that. I don't want my destiny being caught in all these obligations. Things are getting worse, and I don't know what to do."—*Rachel*

What complicates things is that many young women do not share their concerns with anybody else, usually for fear of negative repercussions. Alternatively, if a woman does talk with someone about it, the feedback she may receive is that *she is in the wrong and needs to change.* This environment puts both spouses in a problematic situation because it robs them of the opportunity to grow in their marriage by engaging in respectful, self-confident interpersonal exchange.

Another factor to consider is that in some religions, sacrifice and suffering—pain in some form—are considered a vital part of spiritual growth, religiosity, or being a moral person. *Enduring suffering without complaint is thought of as a virtue.* If a wife is mistreated by her husband and endures this suffering, she may perceive that she will somehow benefit from the situation—either through growth in her inner life, according to her religion, or at least through recognition and appreciation from her family and community.

A further challenge is the problem of ending an abusive or unhealthy relationship when there is *social and religious stigma regarding divorce.* Religious leaders may encourage the victim to stay in her relationship, believing marriage is an inviolable bond, without considering the well-being and the safety of the woman. An additional weight is the expectation of *commitment to family,* with the woman usually being the pillar responsible for family unity and harmony.

Evelyn is a middle-aged woman who is a homemaker and mother of two teenagers. Her husband drinks heavily and becomes aggressive when drunk. Recently he insulted and beat Evelyn, finally locking her out of the house in the middle of the night. Evelyn went to her religious leader for advice. He told her, "Return home and forgive him. He is your husband and the father of your children."

When religious beliefs are used to provide "rationale" for maintaining traditional gender roles, it may exacerbate the problem of gender-based imbalance of power and abuse. However, *religious beliefs can as well be used positively to support good decision-making or provide comfort in difficult times*. So religion can also create solutions to that problem.

Across environments, one of the issues we continue to face is society's tendency to blame the victim for being abused, as though the mistreated person is responsible or did something to warrant the abuser's actions. This is hugely disempowering and harmful to victims and society as a whole. It can result in profound psychological consequences, which affect self-esteem, the motor of the self.

If a woman in a problematic relationship does not have the support of her family and faith community, lacks economic resources, and on top of that believes she has done wrong or is failing to act following her religion's expectations, she may likely ask for her husband's forgiveness and stay in the marriage. She will try to continue working on the relationship, intending to be a better wife, more submissive and obedient.

When the woman is part of a racial, ethnic, sexual, or religious minority, her situation could be more difficult and the pressure more severe, because in addition to being a woman, she is also not part of the dominant culture. Moreover, if she is from a different ethnic or religious background, she also is likely to have a different understanding of societal norms, values, and beliefs.

Religious women and women in religious environments face pressures from without and within. The external forces come from trying to conform to social-religious norms, which include following her husband's guidance. The internal pressures stem from personal struggles to be free of guilt or shame, to restore her self-esteem, to connect with her faith or beliefs, and to forgive.

PERSONAS OF A RELIGIOUS WOMAN

A religious woman may experience or inhabit various personas—a manner in which she identifies or presents herself to others, whether consciously or subconsciously—as she moves through stages and endeavors in her life. Here are a few examples of the personas a religious woman may have. She may portray more than one of these personas at different times in her life.

Convinced

This woman is confident in the rightness of her choices, the goodness of her identity, and her adherence to all religious mandates. She is happy in her family life and an active, supportive member of her religious community. She is a role model to others.

Stella is a devout religious woman, dedicated mother and homemaker. She told me: "I think it's good that there are more options for women these days. Still, for me, *I believe a woman's right career is to be a wife and a mother, devoted to our creator,* as we were taught, and as women before us have done since the beginning of time. I don't understand women who don't want to get married or women who are married but don't want children."

Naïve

This woman is often inexperienced in the ways of the world and tends to trust others, believing the best of them. She expects that if she does what is right, everything will turn out well in the end. She is often dependent on others and does not cultivate personal strength and inner confidence.

Molly's dream was to get married and have her own home, so she was delighted when that happened. She felt she had done the right thing by getting married, so she expected everything to go well. After a few months, Molly noticed her husband acting distracted; he frequently came home late in the evening. She did not ask him any questions or try to communicate about this situation, because she wanted to be a "good wife." *"I know things will change for the better if I do my part,* if I'm patient and pray for him," Molly told me. "Things will go back to how they were at the beginning when I was everything to him."

Passive

This type of woman is so agreeable and submissive that may not realize when someone is taking advantage of her, which puts her at risk of being abused. When she becomes conscious her passivity is connected to the mistreatment or abuse she suffers, she experiences shame and guilt, believing she is solely to blame for the difficult situation she is in.

"Since my earliest memories, I was always a good girl in comparison to my tomboy sister," Rose said. "My parents praised me and criticized her, which taught me that my way was better than hers. I continued to approach all my relationships this way, *finding out what others wanted from me so I could act accordingly.* I think if someone loves me, he or she'll know what is good for me, and they'll appreciate if I follow what they expect. I can't even figure out what to do if I don't have the input from my husband and a few friends."

Victim

This woman suffers from a harmful or abusive relationship but feels helpless to defend herself or change her situation. She, too, has spent much time and energy on being a "good woman." Pleasing others is part of her identity to the point that she does not know if she wants to or can change her behavior.

"My husband is sometimes so distant and indifferent, even verbally and emotionally abusive. I don't work, and we have financial problems constantly. My place is at home—I like being a housewife—and I don't know what I could do if I had to work. I've had bad luck with my choice of husband. But it's impossible for me to think about divorce. We've already been together sixteen years. *Marriage is forever, so it is what it is.*"—*Claire*

Idealistic

These women are convinced that the correct values of life are kindness, acceptance, and submissiveness, as taught in conservative religious environments, and that living up to these ideals is the only way to be happy and fulfilled. Jessica's comments encapsulate this:

"The best part of being a woman is related to our mission in life: to be a wife and a mother. The husband is the head of the house, and if we accept this, we'll be happy. Whatever your husband and children need is fine, because a wife and mother puts others first. Your husband is human and not perfect, *so maybe he won't always respond the way you want. However, if you've done your part, then either way, you'll be in high spirits.*"

Resigned

This woman has fully embraced that "love" is long-suffering, so she is fatalistic and prepared to accept the "inevitable" destiny of women, as laid out by religious leaders and traditions. She serenely tolerates and endures all that comes her way, as a good woman does, confident that this is the only acceptable way to approach life.

"My mother and I are the only women in my family. We never have to make any decisions; we just ask my father what to do. My brothers have authority over me, and they can do and get away with many things I can't. My mother is extremely submissive to my father because if she's ever the least bit independent, he is verbally abusive. I've learned from my mom's example that being submissive and nice reduces conflicts and problems. *She says that patience and resignation are important attributes for a woman,* and the best way to get them is by praying."—*Janet*

Rebellious

Although this woman is defiant and disobedient when it comes to following the norms expected of a good woman, she ultimately complies with them. As a result, she is in constant conflict, struggling between her feelings and behaviors regarding religious norms.

"I hardly think I'm like my mother or grandmother," Sarah told me. "I was single and independent for many years. I worked and did what I liked in my free time." But Sarah struggled to find a partner and felt that her friends, who were more traditional religious women, had excellent husbands and happy marriages.

Even though Sarah believed women and men should have the same freedoms, she concluded that she needed to change her approach to enter into a relationship. She said, *"I'll start by holding my tongue more, hiding my interests and skills, going to services more frequently,* and doing what's expected of a good woman, because I want the validation of having a husband and being a wife."

CLOSING THOUGHTS

Some of the above personas are related to the specific pressures women may experience in religious contexts because of *traditional ideas about gender roles.* Women should be free to develop their lives. We deserve to experience the depth and breadth of the opportunities life has to offer. Our relationships should be built on dynamics that *promote growth and happiness for both partners.*

Of course, *religion can absolutely be a source of solutions and resources for living a better life and improving relationships.* Moreover, many religious communities are slowly becoming more open to applying religious teachings in an evolving, modern context. There is still much work to be done to understand the human consequences of adhering to specific ideas and customs, and *to create space for the natural progress inherent to humanity.*

18

Sexual Minority Women

Sexual minority women (SMWs) are exposed to multiple oppressions, both external and internalized, that complicate their relationships and personal lives. This oppression results from living in a *society that is patriarchal and heterosexist*.

Heterosexism—the belief that men and women should be attracted to the other sex—is associated with prejudice, and negative attitudes and behaviors toward those who are LGBTQ+. The heterosexist attitudes and systems SMWs must navigate within daily life are exacerbated by *internalized heterosexism*, which develops when negative societal attitudes are incorporated into the self. In other words, an SMW may have negative views of herself because of her sexual orientation.

Besides, like other women, SMWs are exposed to the pressures of sexism related to societal beliefs that men are physically, mentally, and emotionally better than women, more competent and trustworthy. Society and families tend to treat men preferentially, often giving boys and men better opportunities as compared with girls and women. Women might be objectified, reducing their value to their beauty, age, and weight.

SMWs may experience some *benefits and advantages* in their personal lives and intimate relationships. Women in same-sex relationships are likely to report greater feelings of autonomy, friendliness, intimacy, and confidence as compared with women in heterosexual relationships.[70,72] They share more activities, and their social life can be rewarding, especially compared to family members or other networks that are unsupportive of their sexual orientation. In general, same-sex partners have a better understanding of each other based on having similar experiences of oppression and more respect because of this fundamental empathy. There may be less of a gender-based power imbalance in female same-sex relationships. These women may be more egalitarian in their roles and feel less restricted than women in relationships with men.[70,71,72]

However, the pressures of sexism and heterosexism and the marginalization of SMWs can *affect personal identity and relationships in negative ways* and lead to psychological distress. SMWs might feel ashamed of their sexual identity because of a lack of societal acceptance, angry about the injustices and barriers they experience, wounded by other people's negative responses, fearful, and unsure whom they can trust. It is tough to be questioned by so many—from family members to people at school, work, church, and other social environments.

These societal pressures affect *identity*, which is the backbone of who we are as individuals and in our interpersonal relationships. Our sense of self is always part of the foundation of all relationships we form in life, including the relationship with ourselves. Experiencing conflict about our identity often leads to psychological distress, which takes on different forms.

"I was always attracted to girls, but I didn't have any lesbian relationships until I was older. When I was a teenager, my mom was constantly telling me, 'Diane, you're a girl! Act like one.' I worried that she suspected something.

"When I was twenty-one, I realized that my feelings for my coworker Audrey went beyond friendship, that I was in love with her, and—happily—that the feelings were mutual. We became a couple. I was happy but conscious that there was a significant obstacle to our happiness: my parents.

"My family had very rigorous religious values. I knew they thought being gay was immoral, wrong, dirty. I had a good relationship with my parents but needed to hide this part of my identity from them. When I finally came out, I was still living at home, and my parents were distraught. A few months after I told my family, my father was diagnosed with pancreatic cancer. I felt miserable, mainly because I'd heard that cancer can be triggered by stress. Was my confession, which caused him unhappiness, part of the reason for his disease?

"My dad was like an impenetrable wall at times. He also refused to acknowledge my relationship with Audrey. The rest of the family was on his side, including my mom, who began using a very combative language with me. I felt like I'd been thrown out of my family.

"Audrey and I decided to move in together, and I chose not to see my family for a while because of how their aggression had escalated. We were delighted together at first. Every day was an adventure for us. But gradually we started feeling lonely. We didn't have many friends, and our families were distant and angry at us. We didn't have much money to spend on activities outside our home. Our relationship started feeling insecure. I felt overwhelmed and exhausted. We began to fight—verbal insults initially, but it got worse, and we sometimes lashed out at each other physically. We knew we had to do something.

"A gay friend helped us find a counselor specializing in LGBT relationships. It took a while to go through our problems and start building a solid foundation for our life. We could see that *being lesbians is how we are, not something we chose, but it didn't mean we couldn't be happy and have a good relationship.*

"My father died almost two years following his diagnosis. After Audrey and I had lived together for over three years, my mother finally visited our home for the first time. She's still distant toward Audrey, but things can change. I love my mom, and I know she feels bad about her past behavior. My family and I started getting closer again, and they attended our wedding last summer. After all that we've been through, I'm proud to say that I'm a happily married woman!"—*Carol*

Even though social conditions have significantly changed over the last three decades, many stereotypes and misconceptions about lesbian and bisexual women still exist. In the next sections, I will outline some of the issues that young and middle-age SMWs may deal with.

YOUNG SEXUAL MINORITY WOMEN

The process of discovery regarding sexual identity—and specifically coming to an understanding and acceptance of a sexual minority identity—can be long and complicated, and affect a young woman profoundly. Some of the reasons are that this process is related to *identity*, the pillar of the self, and this journey is often *solitary*. Girls and young women who realize they do not identify as heterosexual feel different from other girls and worry that they are wrong or not normal. Being different is especially painful during adolescence, a time when we very much need to belong and feel we fit in with our peers. Any differences are perceived as "being less" than those around us.

Once a young woman begins understanding her sexual identity and identifies as a member of a sexual minority, one of the next steps she faces is the journey of *coming out*. This can be extremely hard, especially if she first comes out to a person with whom she has a significant relationship with, such as a parent. It is a highly emotional experience. The young person is expressing something central to her identity, while the listener, receiving unexpected information, may feel unprepared to respond and may even be homophobic. The feedback a young SMW receives to coming out, especially from those she is close to, becomes a formative part of her experience. Conflicts that may arise have to be resolved for the young SMW to continue her developmental journey.

Heterosexual people are almost never put in a position where they are expected to talk about their sexuality and sexual preferences or explain "why" they are heterosexual since heterosexuality is considered the norm. However, for people who are part of a sexual minority, *coming out never ends.* They may repeatedly be put on the spot to disclose their orientation, deal with people's shock and surprise, and answer personal questions about their intimate life. "I always have to come out to new people I meet or when I'm in new situations," an SMW told me. *"What's so annoying is that you never know if it will impact something you want or are trying to do personally or professionally."*

Every SMW will have a coming out story that is unique to her, but many do experience problems or confrontations with their family of origin, especially if the family is traditional or conservative. Even for relatively open-minded and accepting parents, there may still be a period of transition as they process the information their daughter has shared and do their best to support her. Either way, there is usually a clear "*before* and *after* the coming out" for the SMW and her family.

For a young SMW, some of the family's questions or confusion around her coming out could stem from wondering whether *she is old enough to know her sexual orientation definitively*, and thinking it is just a "phase." Some people may believe they can modify a young person's sexual orientation through changing her environment and circle of friends, or that "conversion to heterosexuality" is possible through treatment.

Family members' reactions can also be based on their concern and worry that their daughter will face bullying and harassment at school or socially because of her sexual orientation. The school environment and related social circles are a significant part of teenage life.

Unfortunately, many LGBTQ+ teenagers do suffer harassment and discrimination at school.[73] For that reason, schools often have programs to stop it. As a result, overt bullying is more controlled in these environments. However, bullying and harassment still exist in subtle, perhaps more insidious ways in the form of *microaggressions* (subtly offensive comments or actions)[74] based on stereotypes, prejudices, and stigma against LGBTQ+ people. These microaggressions are mostly verbal, but some involve action, like ignoring a person or not inviting her to events. Even when a behavior is not intentional, the SMW may perceive it as such, because she expects other people to act in discriminatory ways and has become hypersensitive.[74]

The young SMW may also experience painful feelings of isolation as she tries to process and explain feelings that may not be entirely clear yet, even to her. Her parents may be adjusting and unsure of how best to interact with their daughter, sometimes getting it right and other times handling things poorly. The young SMW may feel a lot of confusion and guilt if her family takes her coming out hard and she faces scorn from her peers.

It is helpful for LGBTQ+ youth to meet other teens like them, but this can be difficult. Some LGBTQ+ youth may not be out yet, and there are some legitimate safety concerns with trying to find positive support groups online. A young SMW also faces the challenges of navigating a same-sex relationship with fewer accessible role models.

"I was fifteen when I knew I was lesbian. I'd always had crushes on other girls, never on boys. I was attracted to a good friend of mine, Kelly, and we started talking about how we felt about each other. We thought it was romantic to exchange love letters.

"One day my mom found one of the letters Kelly sent me. She didn't say anything at first, but when my dad arrived, they called me to the kitchen to talk. They said that what I was doing was wrong and they would help me change. They blamed Kelly and said she was a bad influence on me. I told them I was lesbian and nothing would change that. They said I didn't know what I was talking about, that I had to end the relationship, that they felt ashamed of me. *I said 'I didn't kill anybody; I want to be myself, and I'm gay.'*

"At that moment I felt great peace because I was out of the closet. I know they still need to process this. I do, too, because I'm learning about myself all the time. But ultimately, it's all going to work out. *I'm not confused about who I am, and I don't have to lie about or hide my identity.* I can be myself knowing that I'm lesbian and feeling that I'm a good person. Whatever sexual identity I have, it's my responsibility to live my life in the best way I can."—*Judy*

MIDDLE-AGE SEXUAL MINORITY WOMEN

Among older SMWs, there are two main groups: those who have identified as SMW since early in life, and those who became SMW later on. I will start with this second group, as these women face unique challenges.

Women who identify as SMW later in life

Many of these women grew up in environments closed to even considering the prospect of a lesbian sexual identity. However, as the years went by, these women became more aware of this possibility or found they had changed. So they started on an entirely *new journey of discovering themselves and beginning a new phase in their lives.* Many of these women have had traditional family lives and been in relationships with men. Some have been single until this point, while others were exploring different options. Sexuality is fluid. It is an area of human nature and behavior we do not yet fully understand and continue to learn about.

"I started questioning my sexuality in my late thirties. It wasn't as though I'd felt attracted to women and had repressed those feelings. But at some point, *I started to think about myself differently and feel another way about what I wanted,* developing and expanding what was already in me. I started wanting to be closer to one of my female friends, Jane. I thought about things we could do together, like go on a short trip or get into a hobby together. Just thinking of a great friendship, which developed into wanting more physical contact, sleeping side by side but without sex, and then eventually sexual intimacy. The desire for physical contact and sexual intimacy with a woman was met when I started a relationship with Jane. I felt emotional and physical satisfaction like never before. That was when I understood how my sexual identity had developed."—*Christine*

The *coming out* process is always tricky, but it can be more complicated when it happens later in life. First, the woman has established a higher number of interpersonal relationships and networks—for example, a partner or spouse, children, friends, coworkers, and social acquaintances—and has different obligations to these people. How an SMW might disclose her sexual identity would look very different depending on whether she is talking with a partner, child, family member, or colleague. Second, for all the prior years, these people have known and thought of her as straight, a *central characteristic* of identity.[75]

People may have unpredictable reactions to the disclosure, depending on their personalities, their own experiences and stage of life, and their relationship with the SMW. Some people react in supportive, affirming ways. Others are offended or disbelieving. Some ask inappropriate questions and push for details. "I was surprised by the things people said to me when I came out," Heather told me. "An old friend, who is also very religious, told me how 'unacceptable' my 'lifestyle' is. Other friends asked me for details about very personal aspects of my sex life, as though this were 'juicy gossip.' Another friend responded that *I'd better not try anything with her.*"

For a woman who identifies as an SMW later in life, the surprise, questions, and opinions can feel overwhelming and even like personal attacks. *"How could you decide something like this when you've had a normal life?* What about your husband? What about your *kids?* Or your old friends?" It can be exhausting and painful for the SMW to face these varied reactions and answer people's questions, especially if she is still working things out herself. Besides, there are other potential repercussions she may experience in her personal or professional life.

There are new changes to adapt to, like how comfortable she feels showing affection in public to a same-sex partner. She may have previously felt relaxed doing so with boyfriends or a husband but is now more cautious in relationships with women, unsure of how others will react or perceive her.

She may also face questions from the lesbian community, possibly even judgment and exclusion. They may be suspicious that she will return to her previous lifestyle, or create confusion and suffering in her partners while she works on resolving her inner conflicts and questions.

People often think the woman has been "lying" to herself and others about her sexuality. Actually, the woman might have known for a while that she was not straight but opted for a heterosexual life in order to avoid the problems she would face if she disclosed her (new) sexual identity. *Cultural expectations have a remarkable influence on people's deci-*

sions. Of course, a better understanding of sexual identity and self can also be part of the woman's journey, until she finally comes to the point where she is ready to accept and acknowledge herself more authentically.

Others think that women who were previously in relationships with men but now want a same-sex relationship are making this change not because of their sexual identity but because there was something wrong in their previous heterosexual relationship. In other words, maybe that specific man was not the right one for them or something negative happened in that particular relationship. *"Why not try a relationship with another man?"* many people will ask. This type of thinking shows the influence of heterosexism.

"I lived with my boyfriend, Ron, for almost three years. We have a daughter, and we had a happy, stable life together. But *something was niggling in my mind that I didn't want even to think about, and that was picturing myself with another woman.* I was scared of these feelings, and every time I imagined being with a woman, I would make love with Ron to try to forget this growing interest and desire. As time passed, having sex with Ron wasn't enough to make me forget my fantasies with women. I started going to gay bars, and one night, I met Carrie. It was a magical moment! We started a relationship almost immediately, and I can say that I am now happy."—*Ruth*

Women who identify as SMWs later in life and are in a heterosexual relationship may bring it to a close before entering the world of same-sex dating and relations. However, some take a different approach— they stay in their marriage or relationship with a man while exploring their newly discovered sexuality.

"I know that full honesty comes with a price, and not everyone wants to pay it. In my opinion, it's OK to stay quiet about my sexual attraction and keep it for myself. What is coming out going to get me? *I might lose everything I've worked hard for.* My other life is mine alone. *Nobody judges or ridicules or excludes me because of something as personal as whom I'm attracted to.*"—Joan

Women who identify as SMW earlier in life

Women who identify as SMWs earlier in life may or may not be out but have had a pretty good understanding of their sexual identity since their youth or adolescence. Some women in this group opted to remain entirely or partially in the closet, especially in their faith community or workplace, because the social pressures of heterosexism are powerful, and they are at risk of experiencing negative consequences, such as discrimination, exclusion, aggression, and bullying.

Many of these women had awkward or difficult adolescence and young adulthood phases but are growing into greater confidence and strength, and they enjoy their life. Work has been a consistent pillar in their lives because they realized early on that they needed to be self-sufficient. While they face the same limitations and inequities that other women do, there are some differences. These SMWs are likely to have worked more consistently than traditional women, mainly because they have not perceived marriage and motherhood as the ultimate goal; or, if they are parents, they and their partner have better balance regarding childcare and household chores.

CLOSING THOUGHTS

Women who are attracted to other women face unique barriers in a patriarchal, heterosexist society. These barriers are particularly substantial in conservative circles, such as religious, ethnic, and rural communities. SMWs may be perceived as different or odd just because of their sexual orientation, and they often face many questions about, and adverse reactions to, their identity. The challenge for SMWs is to rise above these barriers, empowered by the knowledge that *a woman's life is her own, whatever her sexual identity, and she has a right to make her own choices.*

Although social acceptance of other sexual orientations is growing, SMWs still experience judgment and discrimination. This may come about in subtle but pervasive ways affecting the woman's life and relationships. Every SMW I have met has examples of negative reactions regarding her sexual orientation—from people becoming distant, or advising them to "*think about what you're doing,*" to condemning their "immorality." Almost all the women I interviewed spoke of *the judgment they felt from others, especially from other women.*

I asked them what message they wanted to express to others, and the pith of it is this: "Maybe you don't agree with my reality, but don't judge me. Please don't put me down and yourself on a pedestal. When you act as if being heterosexual makes you superior to me and 'good,' what I hear is that being me and being different is 'bad.' *Respect my identity, and try to understand me.*"

This sentiment is the foundation for how we should approach all our interpersonal relationships. Our interactions should be rooted in understanding, respect, and unfailing acceptance of each other's decisions and choices.

PART 3

INTERSECTIONS OF POWER
AND SOCIAL PRESSURES IN
WOMEN'S LIVES

In the first part of this book, I talked about the pressures society places on women. In this last section, I will describe how these social pressures intersect with power dynamics to open the door to *restrictions, limitations, criticism, shame and guilt, unhealthy comfort zones, objectification, and benevolent sexism.* These connected factors can *limit women from developing influence and power* in themselves and in the circles they touch.

Power is the freedom to make decisions, the ability to make things happen and to influence others so they act in line with our purposes. We possess power when we have a real sense of who we are, and that what we bring is strong and capable. There are stereotypes linked to power, however. It implies assertiveness, courage, and guts—qualities typically associated with masculinity. Women are expected to be "nice," and many consider power and kindness different paths.

Another word we use to talk about power is *ambition*—wanting to be more, do more, and have more; being driven and hungry. Being ambitious is not often correlated with being feminine. This is something we can change.

Patriarchal ideology, which sees women as inferior, concentrates power in men's hands. With that in mind, the way women access resources is by conforming to the expectations of those holding power. Because being compliant is a way to gain resources, it is also a way for women to feel they have some control.

A woman may achieve some power if she is highly educated and experienced. However, *sexism is still at play* as, in many cases, a woman needs to demonstrate more knowledge and capacity than a man to merit consideration. Women born into wealth or influential families can exert a type of power, but generally it still is less than that of the men in their family. In the domestic realm, women have some power at home, but it may be limited to areas that feel less important—cleaning, home decor, and what's for dinner.

The social pressures that affect women's potential, ambitions, and power are not insurmountable. That they exist does not mean women cannot garner power, but doing so takes more effort and willpower on our part. If you want more in your life and spheres of influence, *having awareness of how social pressures act as a barrier can help you to plan and act smarter.*

19

How Social Pressures Restrict Women's Power

Whether we look at political, economic, religious, or civic leadership roles, we can see many examples of women's exclusion from positions of power and influence. We see this even in women's personal lives. I believe this imbalance of power is the reason women experience so many social pressures. Some may see this in reverse: that social pressures are what limit women's ability to have and maintain power, or that women lose what power they have as a result of complying with limiting social pressures.

What came first, the chicken or the egg? Pressures because of the absence of power, or lack of power because of pressures? Either way, we go back to the issue of power. Power is something many women do not have much of, or only have within prescribed limits, such as the home. *They may not know it is okay to reach for power.* This means *women are often subject to the power and influence of a patriarchal society,* with its many expectations and resultant pressures for how women should be, behave, think and feel. So, because of socialization, internalizing pressures, or limited role models, many women are convinced that *trying to keep up with these expectations is the right thing to do.*

What about women who have some power? They often perceive it as *a personal accomplishment due to their unique skills or circumstances.*

As a result, they might not recognize that their experience is relevant to other women. Thus, they do not act as role models or help other women gain power. They might think there is no way to replicate their success or teach other women to have influence as well.

Of course, there are women with power who are working hard to lift other women up. However, being a woman makes the road to success more complicated. For example, women often need twice the level of knowledge and capabilities as men to be considered for the same position.

What about women who have visible roles but lack authentic power? They may gossip and criticize women who do have power as being far from the ideal. They also enforce rigid routines over some situations, like running a home, maintaining household routines, and so on. They show a type of power, albeit limited and disconnected from determining more far-reaching outcomes.

What about women who are headed toward gaining some power? They are often exhausted because they do not know what to choose, so they pick what seems the best of all possibilities. This scattered approach is the opposite of power. Authentic, robust power is developed by preparing yourself internally and externally to move in a precise direction that influences yours and others' lives.

HOW SOCIAL PRESSURES CAN AFFECT WOMEN HAVING POWER

The social pressures women face are connected to power structures in a system that can significantly limit and restrict women's lives. Following are some specific examples:

Pressure to be beautiful, thin, and youthful

The pressure on women to be beautiful, thin, and young according to societal expectations *concentrates women's value and power in their physical appearance.* How we look is a big part of creating first impressions.[76] A beautiful, well-put-together presentation is an advantage in our society, but it is *not enough* to sustain long-term relationships. There can even be *downsides* to being beautiful and attractive, as people may assume the woman lacks intelligence or substance. So, while a pleasant appearance can help make a good first impression, women absolutely need *to cultivate and tap into their inner strengths and other resources for real success and power.*

Pressure to be perfect

The pressure to be perfect robs us of opportunities to gain and demonstrate power because to achieve success we need to be open to trial, error, and imperfection. Power involves creativity, drive, intensity, energy, and strength in dealing both with familiar and unexpected situations. This requires the willingness to take risks and not beat ourselves up over mistakes we have made.

A healthier mindset acknowledges that failure is part of life; that we can explore mistakes to increase learning and experience. We cannot access new capabilities and resources if we are under constant pressure to think, feel, and act according to someone else's definition of "perfection." Our focus will be on copying established methods and trying to follow "proven" paths to success, rather than asking questions, learning, and seeking out the new. *The pressure of perfection restricts us, which is the opposite of what we need to pursue and gain power.*

Pressure to be subordinate

The pressure to be subordinate is most likely to occur in a relational context. It happens when the woman accepts, from the onset, that she comes second and that the other person in the relationship holds all the power. *We have no power when we allow this pressure.* In this environment, it is possible the woman feels judged by her partner—that she is lesser, not good enough, or not doing satisfactorily. She may experience deep shame and guilt as a result.

This woman not only loses her power and freedom of individual expression but might feel she needs to act more like the person holding power to improve her standing with him. Her partner may also objectify her in exchange for the sense of "comfort," status, and security he offers her. *These situations leave women powerless, vulnerable, and dependent.* They often lose sight of their self-worth and are unable to see other options or possibilities.

Pressure to get married

We limit the power of our potential if we give in to the trouble to get married or commit to a long-term relationship when that is not really what we want, or we are not sure, or we are not ready. We let everything else in life take second place to the idea of finding "the one" who will give us the fairytale ending women and girls hear so much about from society.

Family and friends can put a lot of pressure on us to be in relationships or to get married. However, that can lead to situations where the more we try, the less authentic we are, and the more rejections we face. *Desperation to find a partner becomes our driving force, and we lose the power of our other strengths, qualities, and potential.*

Pressure to have children

The pressure placed on women to have children as part of being a "real woman" affects women's ability *to self-determine their present and future.* Women should have the power to decide whether having a child is an option they want to explore.

The traditional view has been that a woman's destiny is to be a mother. This view is becoming less pervasive but can still be an intense pressure for women in conservative environments, because community members may gauge a woman's virtue and worth by whether she is a mother. Women who are voluntarily childless often face many perplexing questions and negative opinions related to their decision.

Having a child has a significant bearing on the type of life a person has on a day-to-day and long-term basis. *A woman's life is her own, and how she wants to live it is subject to her power and choices.*

Pressure not to divorce

The pressure to stay married no matter what *limits a woman's power to determine her future and keeps her tied to a decision made in the past* when perhaps the woman, or her partner, or the circumstances were different. A woman may feel this pressure through the negative images often associated with divorce, such as "destroying your family," "damaging your children," and "doing the opposite of what society, family, and your faith hold to be right."

This pressure affects a woman's power because it focuses on the well-being of everyone around her who may be affected by the divorce, but it *does not consider the woman's best interests and the price she pays: losing her happiness, safety, and peace by remaining in an unfortunate marriage.*

Pressure to be a "good woman"

To be a "good woman," you have to forget yourself and put the needs and expectations of others first. When women accept this view as a way of life, *they lose their power*. First, their hard work and self-sacrifice are expected and so go unnoticed. Secondly, as they minimize or ignore self-care, their potential is devalued.

In the good woman role, *the only power a woman has comes from being the "victim."* In other words, she deserves some notice because others make her suffer and do not appreciate what she does for them. This is a *negative power* because it does not lead to growth. It implies that others are to blame and there is nothing the woman needs to change.

Pressure to be heterosexual

The pressure to be heterosexual dramatically reduces the power of an LGBTQ+ person because *this pressure hits at the core of who we are*. Sexual orientation is not a matter of mere preference; it is an *identity*, an essential part of who a person is.

So for women who identify as LGBTQ+, heterosexist pressures go against their identity. If we cannot develop and maintain our identity, our chances of developing power are immediately limited. *To be influential in the world around us, we must first be powerful within ourselves.*

Pressure to have it all

The pressure to have it all pushes women to the limits of their energy and resources. It *sets up an unrealistic expectation of what power is*: women are seen as powerful if they can have it all, be perfect, and do things flawlessly from the beginning. These are impossible goals; they can be accomplished in part, but only with enormous effort and often under great tension—an *unsustainable workout.*

Power requires *focus.* Also, to have power in a specific area, we need *to grow in that subject,* which means we need to develop the right resources, build capacity, and get experience. *If we act without focus or ability, trying to do many things at once, we will fail in something for sure.* Plus, unrealistic expectations can lead to loss of self-esteem and self-confidence.

Pressure to be silent when exposed to sexual harassment

An imbalance of power that generally considers women to be inferior is at the root of sexual harassment as well as to the pressure to be silent when exposed to it. The pressure to be silent happens because the other party may exert his power against the woman, putting her at risk for great loss—not only of her job and career future but also her well-being and peace of mind.

She may be subjected to judgment, embarrassment, and blame for what happened, which can lead to feelings of shame and vulnerability. The possibility of paying a high price for not remaining silent *is very real for women.*

Pressure not to opt out of your career

Being a "career woman," especially if you are on a successful career path, can feel like the "right thing to do." However, the pressure to keep on pursuing a career can also interfere when you are exploring other options. You may want to get married, have a child, or raise your kids, and any of these life changes can affect your interests, resources, and time.

Staying on a career path based on external pressure can be detrimental to your power if you are acting out of sync with your current motivation, the driving force of power. Life does not follow a single, predetermined route. If your circumstances have changed, and you feel inspired and enthusiastic about trying another path, it may be good *to let go of career pressures for a time to pursue your other goals.* We need to respect our interests and motivations, and the seasons in our lives. Each new season will bring with it opportunities and the means to meet them.

IN CONCLUSION

We can see that social pressures limit us, and make it extremely challenging to develop and express power. *The more we try to live up to societal pressures, the less power we have.* By not letting them dictate our lives, the more powerful we will be in what we can control and set up.

Your life is your own, and it is right for you to have the power to determine your path. This is not selfishness. Yes, you may have obligations to your family, partner, children, parents, friends, and society, but *your first responsibility is to yourself.* Blindly following others' expectations damages you and your power.

Self-care is about what you want and need—not what others want you to do. This is linked to power, because taking control of our lives means making decisions to change our circumstances, embark on new paths, endure, and be resilient even when our chosen course is challenging. Self-care makes it possible for us to recharge, take stock, and be true to ourselves.

When you tap into your power and factor what you want and need into your decisions, you will encounter like-minded people who are heading the same way you are, who share common interests. You will be living more genuinely, and the experiences and relationships you cultivate will give you greater satisfaction. *Living authentically is living in freedom.*

20

How Criticism From Other Women Weakens Women's Power

All too often, women are on the receiving end of judgment and criticism. Whether it comes from friends or strangers, at home, in social circles, or the workplace, this judgment often takes the shape of bullying or gossip. When we judge others, we feel superior to them. Pointing out others' mistakes, or even just differences, lets us think that our way of doing things is better, so we must be in the right.

A particular type of criticism women face is the judgment from other women. On the one hand, *women are expected or pressured to be and act in a specific way to match society's expectations.* On the other hand, *women are judged if they move in perfect accordance with those pressures or give them too much sway in their lives.*

For instance, the more beautiful a woman is, the more she is scrutinized. *What about her is real or fake? What is she doing or sacrificing to look so great? Is she following a diet, having surgery, or undergoing special treatments?* She might be viewed with envy, and the rumor mill will dig into all the possible resources this "selfish" woman is using on herself.

The more a woman seems to have everything together, the more she is analyzed and dissected, because it is "impossible" anyone could be that flawless—certainly not without provoking some bitterness. The gossip may be that this woman is not that great: rather, *she's "arrogantly showing off" the best of herself.*

The more dependent on others a woman is, the more she will be judged as *out of sync with present-day realities, too influenced by patriarchal ideas, too distant from feminist principles, too weak to fight for herself or step outside her comfort zone.*

The more success a woman has in her career, the more likely she will face criticism that she *is "self-centered" or has disregarded a woman's "true" priorities of family and children.* Other women may say she got her position with the help of influential men, or that she was ruthless in pursuing her ambitions and climbing the ladder.

The more of a "good woman" a lady is, the more she may face disapproval for *doing nothing for herself, sacrificing too much for her husband and children, putting duty and obligation above pleasure.* She is criticized because she is "too good" to be happy and too far from what is acceptable these days.

There is intense pressure on women to get married or find an acceptable long-term partner. However, a woman who is eager to find a stable relationship is often criticized as being *"desperate."*

With the pressure to have children, if a woman decides to have more than two children or have her children close together, she *may be considered irresponsible.* Other women may question how she raises her kids or say she is making life difficult for her husband since he has to provide for their growing family.

There is pressure on women not to get divorced, but if a woman stays in a difficult marriage, she is criticized for that, too. *She lacks courage, is too dependent or needy to make a life for herself, or is too "high maintenance" to quit her relationship.*

There is pressure to be heterosexual. However, if a woman who has identified as lesbian shows interest in a man, she is criticized as not being *gay "enough," or untrue to herself, or has no idea of what she wants.*

A woman who has an adequate balance in her life and seems to "have it all" is exposed to criticism. Instead of celebrating her strengths, people will try to find fault—*she has it too good, too easy; there must be something wrong about her; she must be hiding something.*

The more independent and less traditional a woman is, the more she becomes a subject for gossip. She is viewed as *self-centered and eccentric* because of the unexpected ways in which she responds to life stages and situations.

As you can see, when a woman follows social pressures, other women may censure her. It's like the saying *"damned if you do, damned if you don't."* Live your life the way society says is right or convenient, but if you do it too well, you will be criticized.

One consequence of this is that women *may not show themselves or their accomplishments and strengths as they are.* Instead, they try to present themselves according to the expectations of the particular group of people they engage with or the circumstances they face. So, *women may show different faces in various settings.*

For example, with a group of acquaintances who are housewives or retired, a successful career woman might not talk about trips or professional events, but about the last recipe she tried.

When chatting with women who are professionals, a "good woman" will talk about time with her husband or children rather than the effort she puts into managing her responsibilities to her family and putting her own needs and desires on the back burner.

A woman who tries to do everything correctly and feels she is keeping on top of things will adjust her conversation to highlight her inadequacies and limitations when talking with another woman going through difficult times.

Women try to match their conversation and presentation to the particular characteristics of their social group *to avoid being criticized behind their back.* The more a woman shows her successes, the more destructive the gossip may be. As a result, when talking with other females, women often *downplay their achievements*, whether in their career, family, or personal life. (An exception to this is interactions with real friends. Many women do, of course, have true friends who are happy for their successes and share in their joy).

ENVY

Why the tendency to want to tear down someone who is doing well? If a woman has or does something we like, we can respond in a few ways. We can be happy for her successes. We can try to replicate what she did because we want what she has. Alternatively, we can feel *envy*: we can try to diminish or even destroy her achievement because we want what she has *but* fear we are incapable of doing something similar. When another woman succeeds, we might feel like she is showing us up as a failure. So we feel pain and discomfort—*unless we put down the other woman's achievement.*

Envy is a negative emotion common in interpersonal interactions. It is the feeling that if we cannot have something, nobody should have it. It is at the root of "wishing" that other women be unsuccessful so that we feel better about not doing well.

Envy is harmful. It makes us actively wish for other women to fail or feel happy when one of them faces a setback, so that we can feel better about ourselves. This happens not only in the workplace or casual social circles, but in close ones too—between sisters, mothers and daughters, and close friends. Cheryl and Barbara's stories are examples of some of the ways women experience envy.

"My friend was having a tough time in her marriage, and she and her husband planned a trip to spend time together and try to resolve their differences. As the date of their return neared, I found myself *wishing that they were unable to resolve things and ended their relationship.* I felt terrible about these thoughts, but I couldn't stop them. I feel very ashamed for thinking and feeling this way, but I couldn't avoid it."—*Cheryl*

"My sister Tara has a great family life. I don't. My husband drinks too much, and my oldest son is bipolar, so we face a lot of challenges. Tara's family looks perfect. She and her husband have a good relationship. They don't seem to have any major problems. Last month Tara was promoted to a higher-level position. *I had secretly been hoping she wouldn't get it.* I feel like a horrible sister, and that makes me feel worse about my problems."—*Barbara*

Thoughts and feelings of envy are part of the expression of *our complex and imperfect human nature.* If you have ever felt envious of someone, you are not alone. Even so, we should be aware that envy is a destructive force. *Envy underlies gossip and judging others.*

- In social circles, if we feel envious of other women who are more beautiful, fun, cool, articulate, or assertive than us, we use gossip to level the playing field—putting them down helps us feel better.

- In work relationships, where we may be threatened by the capabilities, degrees, or positions of other women, we find fault and gossip to question their merits.
- In close personal relationships, we are often more aware of both the similarities and differences between us, and it is easy to think, "Why her and not me?"

As Barbara's story shows, another way in which envy is harmful is that it often leads to *feelings of shame.* We feel terrible about our envious thoughts and feelings, that they make us a "bad" person. This becomes internalized: *"It's no wonder things aren't working out when I have these bad thoughts."*

WHY A DEFENSIVE WOMAN TENDS TO GOSSIP MORE

When a woman derives a lot of social statuses and personal security from her comfort zone, she will work hard to make sure *nothing puts it at risk.* This woman does not feel secure or confident in herself; she feels she has a lot to lose, so she is defensive. *If she appreciates and acknowledges other women, she risks her sense of security.* She cannot afford to have anyone else at her level.

By criticizing others and pointing out their flaws, she *elevates herself and secures her position.* Gossiping and tearing others down gives her a sense of superiority, which provides her with pleasure and a sense of power. It is a way to get back at those who are stepping outside their comfort zones—something she is afraid to do—and achieving more as a result.

IN CONCLUSION

Envy can complicate the social pressures women face. A woman may try to comply with social expectations and show she is doing so, while at the same time be dismissive of her strengths because she does not want to become the center of envy, criticism, and gossip. *Trying to play both sides of this field can disorient us.*

Envy is a negative, divisive force that paralyzes our progress—this is something we need to be conscious of. However, we do not have to feel bad if envious emotions come our way. We are not responsible for our thoughts or feelings, *only for how we choose to respond to them.* We cannot control every thought, but we can change the channel and select positive actions toward ourselves and others. For example, we can *decide not to let envious thoughts become criticism and gossip of other women who are happy and doing well.* We can recognize that another woman's success *does not diminish our own* and that there will be other opportunities for us to shine.

The way to stop the adverse effects of envy is to understand where it comes from and how it can hurt us and others. From this position of honest *self-awareness*, we can open the door to positive forces that will strengthen us: understanding, cooperation, support, solidarity, and teamwork.

21

Shame And Guilt

One of the reasons societal pressures are so harmful is that *they leave us with feelings of deep shame and guilt*, which become intertwined with many of the challenges women face.

Regarding gender stereotypes, we may receive benefits if we follow them (for example, social acceptance) or experience disadvantages if we deviate from them (for instance, rejection). Gender stereotypes, which usually express an ideal in its most perfect form, *generate high expectations*. Nevertheless, we are human, with all the limitations that come with this. It is unrealistic for us to think we can live up to the level of these expectations, yet we still struggle with *feeling embarrassed, guilty, and ashamed when we fall short.*

Many of the women I have spoken to over the years said one of the main reasons *they acted according to gender-specific social pressures was to avoid feeling shame or guilt.* As I already mentioned, shame is feeling that you as a person are not good enough, that you are a mistake. Guilt is the sense you have done something wrong, that you made an error, and involves regrets and remorse for not doing more or better.[77]

Shame and guilt decrease our self-esteem and self-worth, and this slows us down. We feel we have disgraced ourselves and are not worthy to keep trying, to start afresh. The embarrassment we feel alongside shame and guilt is usually provoked by social criticism that whatever has gone wrong is our fault and happened because we did not act at the level of the ideal, as a good woman should.

THE CONNECTION BETWEEN SHAME/GUILT AND GROWTH

We often face pressure to do things flawlessly, without making a single mistake, even if it is something we have never done before. This pressure creates a lot of fear and tension, which *limits our creativity and growth*. We may also become hypervigilant regarding our actions and presentation, careful of not carrying out something that would embarrass us or show people we do not know what we are doing. The negative, self-denigrating feelings come if we feel that we have disappointed others and failed to live up to their expectations. That society has this unrealistic expectation of perfection gives others a platform to belittle and disrespect us.

Michelle had been married for almost twenty years when she sought counseling. Her friends would tell you she is neither happy nor unhappy in her marriage—happiness has never been a factor in the equation. Michelle and her husband had built certain rituals over the years, things they did together daily, every few months, or on their annual vacations. Michelle was reluctant at first to talk about her marriage; she tried to avoid the topic by saying, "everything is going okay."

The reality was that her husband was psychologically abusive, humiliating and degrading her, especially when she needed his help or support. He often told her she was stupid, neglectful, and thoughtless. *She believed he was right, that she was these negative things, and felt ashamed.* She assumed that if she could change, her husband would be good with her.

She was too embarrassed to tell her friends what was going on, worried that they thought the same things about her. She also felt shame that she could not stand up to her husband. So, again, it was "her fault" she was treated poorly. *She blamed herself for the state of her married life* and kept trying to act in perfect accordance with what she thought was expected of her.

Beverly's story is another example: Her husband is a doctor and began a relationship with one of his colleagues at the hospital. Instead of feeling betrayed, Beverly felt shame that she was not attractive or enough as a woman to keep his interest. "It's my fault he's started a relationship with someone else. *I feel like a failure as a woman but also just in general, like I don't have anything good to offer,"* Beverly said.

Shame and guilt are painful emotions that cause us to close ourselves off to others and to experiences that can bring *healing, growth, and progress into our lives.* We try to hide the problem from others, which makes it almost impossible to get support. We blame ourselves for what we think went wrong and turn ourselves into the victim. Because our self-worth has taken a hit, we often evaluate ourselves adversely.

Others who are insecure themselves may use our mistakes as an opportunity to judge or gossip. This spreads negativity, and it becomes a vicious cycle. *Nobody wins when people are made to feel ashamed and guilty for their efforts or errors, or when these events are turned into fuel for gossip.*

HOW SOCIAL PRESSURES CAN LEAD TO FEELINGS OF SHAME AND GUILT

In part one of this book, I talked about several pressures society places on women. In this section, I will describe how the struggle to comply with society's unrealistic expectations and pressures can lead to feelings of shame and guilt.

Pressure to be beautiful, thin, and youthful

Keeping up with the demand to always look a certain way takes much effort and leads to deep frustration because the reflection staring back at us from the mirror rarely seems like a fashion model. What we tell ourselves is, *"I'm so far behind how I should and want to look. I should eat more appropriately. I should have a better exercise routine. I should do more."* Moreover, when we can't, we blame ourselves and think, *"I'm the problem. I'm not good enough."* We feel shame.

Almost all the women I know have felt that pressure to be beautiful, thin, and youthful and can relate to the scenario I describe here. This pressure is detrimental to our psychological well-being and can lead to many body image and health problems. Instead of falling for a cookie-cutter approach to beauty, we need to realize that our bodies and faces are unique and beautiful just as they are. *We do not have to be ashamed or go to such great (sometimes even dangerous) lengths to change our appearance.*

Pressure to be perfect

The pressure to be perfect—the notion that we can live up to every single unrealistic expectation placed on us, and do it all simultaneously—often leads directly to feelings of shame and guilt.

We are inherently flawed humans and can never be perfect or do everything correctly. But then again, when this is the standard we set for ourselves, and we make a mistake, we are very hard on ourselves.

Instead of realizing that perfection is impossible, we blame ourselves and feel ashamed.

Pressure to be subordinate

Women who experience the pressure to be subordinate to, or dependent on, a man or others often feel much shame and guilt, especially if they want to be more independent or pursue other possibilities. This is the opposite of what is expected, in which the "right thing" to do is to take a second place. So they wonder if their desires are wrong and if that makes them a faulty person. At the same time, they may also feel bad that they are not in the line of advancing equity and freedom of choice for women, and instead accepting lower positions.

If anything negative happens in a relationship with unequal power dynamics—one where the expectation is subordination—*women will probably feel shame and guilt.* They may think that they are not good enough and provoked the problem.

Pressure to get married

I have interacted with many single women who felt ashamed that they were not married or did not have a partner, and internalized this to mean *there was something wrong with them.* They blamed themselves and felt other people also censured and criticized them because they were single.

This was embarrassing and led to self-questioning about why they could not find a partner yet. *What did I do wrong? Do I look desperate? Am I not trying enough or not going about things the right way?* Instead, they should be evaluating their situation more realistically: *Relationships involve two people, and I haven't found the right partner yet. I'm not interested in living with another person. I have other priorities in life.*

Pressure to have children

There is an old stereotype that a woman is not a "real woman" until she has a child. If a woman does not want to have children, there's "*something wrong with her*," and she should *be ashamed because she does not have the desire that defines womanhood.*

Because we have internalized the criticism around the decision to be childless, women who choose that for voluntary, health, or other reasons often need to overcome a wall of internal pressure. In addition to self-blame, the woman may also grapple with pressure from family members or her religious community, provoking *feelings of guilt, regret, and remorse.*

Pressure not to divorce

The pressure not to divorce is linked to wanting to avoid situations that can be painful and cause *feelings of guilt*, such as: hurting our children, changing family relationships permanently, and going against what society and religion say is "right."

Women often blame themselves for not doing the right things to preserve the relationship or feel they are at fault for the mistakes that led to the end of the marriage. With all these negative emotions, they might *see themselves as "not being good enough," which leads to deep shame and embarrassment.*

Pressure to be a "good woman"

The pressure to be a "good woman" creates an expectation that a woman will always put everyone else's needs before her own. *The shame and guilt come in those moments when we want to prioritize our life and needs but feel that this is because we are selfish and conceited.*

Pressure to be heterosexual

If you identify as LGBTQ+, you may have felt the pressures of heterosexism and related shame and guilt. This comes from a patriarchal ideology that men are best and have the most to offer regarding attractiveness and opportunities; so if a woman is not paying attention to men, there must be *something wrong* with her. Women who are coming to terms with their sexual identity may feel shame: *I don't have that attraction, what's wrong with me? Alternatively, they may feel guilty about their attraction to same-sex partners and blame themselves.*

Pressure to have it all

Why do women work so hard to "have it all?" *Because we think that if we can get to that place of having it all, there will be nothing that can make us feel ashamed or guilty.* Otherwise, if one of the big aspects of life seems to be missing—for example, no partner or kids; no career goals; not a lot of friends; a perceived lack of beauty or fitness—we are likely to hear many comments that leave us feeling shame and guilt, unless we are ready with excuses or a plan to fix the "problem."

Kimberly almost has it all, except that she does not have children. This is a decision she and her husband made early in their relationship. When Kimberly meets new people, they often ask why she has no kids. To avoid feeling shame or guilt and to stop the questions, Kimberly tells people that having kids is something she and her husband are "considering" for the future.

Pressure to be silent when exposed to sexual harassment

There is a lot of *shame, guilt, and embarrassment* connected with the experience of sexual harassment. The woman may feel that what happened is somehow her fault, perhaps because of how she dresses or behaves. If the harassment occurred in the workplace, she might worry that if she does not stay quiet, she will lose her job or face other negative repercussions. She may also fear that sexual harassment happened because she is not capable of holding a position or working at a certain level—in other words, because she is somehow *inadequate*.

The woman often feels that decisions about how to adjudicate sexual harassment are out of her hands and that she has no power in the situation. This can also leave her *feeling guilty that she should be stronger or smarter, better able to take care of herself.*

Pressure not to opt out of your career

When women in a career track decide to make a change in their lives—for instance, to stay home to raise their children—they often face a lot of pushback and pressure. They might feel bad that *they are not doing their part to advance women's rights for equity.* They might *feel shame that they are returning to an "old way of life"*—when staying home to raise a family was all women did because their potential and other opportunities were limited.

They might worry that *other women will look down on them*—and some women will. Many women today are fully invested in their independence and the benefits it affords them, so their criticism may come from this angle. Older women's cautions may arise from their personal experience of restricted opportunities and being dependent on a husband. When the pressure comes from both sides of the aisle, *it is easy to feel guilty, that we must be doing something wrong.*

IN CONCLUSION

We can see how social pressures create a slippery slope, *arousing the negative feelings of shame and guilt that damage self-esteem and confidence.* If we can connect the gender-specific expectations we face back to their origin—that is, the social pressures that come from patriarchy and sexism—we can start letting go of these negative feelings toward ourselves.

We can learn to accept that *we are not failing, so we do not need to give in to shame or guilt.*

22

Comfort Zones

Because women are still relegated to second-place status in many parts of the world, some may conclude that a quicker, surer way to access resources and gain respect is to get married or establish a stable relationship with a man. This path may automatically give them a certain sense of security, safety, and control—*a comfort zone*—instead of continually struggling to gain respect and independence through education and competing against men for better-paying jobs.

Some women take this path as an alternative to putting in the effort to develop personal resources. *They align themselves with a man and enjoy all the benefits that come with being in a relationship.* This is particularly the case if they marry a wealthy man; there may be many material advantages, such as a beautiful house, a fancy car, gorgeous clothes, overseas vacations, and a fabulous social life.

WHAT IS A COMFORT ZONE?

A comfort zone is a personal place of safety, security, protection, and control over our physical and emotional environment. As humans, we have an innate need for a sense of safety and control as part of feeling whole.[78,79]

TWO WAYS OF DEVELOPING A COMFORT ZONE

There are two broad ways to develop a comfort zone: We can build our comfort zone based on *internal strength and personal accomplishments*, or we can seek out a comfort zone that comes from an *external source*—for example, through a spouse or partner. Usually, some combination of internal and external factors go into creating a comfort zone, but people may draw more from one side or the other. If a comfort zone comes primarily from within, it is more fully under *our* control. If it comes from a relationship with a man and there is a *power imbalance*, he may have more command, which enables him *to set expectations and precedents for the woman.*

The *external-source* comfort zone usually comes with *a price*: the woman may feel she has little or no room to express herself or ask questions, fearing that challenging her partner could cost her whatever *sense of safety and control the relationship gives her.* The most common example is when a woman finds out her husband is cheating on her. She contemplates whether to confront him and risk changing or ending the relationship, or turn a blind eye to it. Ultimately, she might choose to say nothing because she realizes she has more to lose—her comfortable life and the circumstances she enjoys, not to mention the shame she might bear. How we are judged and evaluated by our peers affects how we think of ourselves, which is part of feeling shame. Often the social blame for the end of a relationship or a divorce falls on the woman: *her partner provided so much for her, so where did she go wrong?*

Many women stay in problematic or abusive relationships, even at the risk of their safety, because of *fear of the unknown.* Even when a comfort zone is not that comfortable—because it is unhealthy—the harmful situation they know seems better than the unfamiliar risks and challenges of leaving that comfort zone. So they stay in them for a long time or even the rest of their life, enduring a problematic situation, *keeping their reality a secret, feeling ashamed, and blaming themselves.* Some women will end the abusive relationship but quickly find themselves in other negative circumstances because they lack self-esteem and aren't confident of being by themselves.

Many women's identities are linked to being in a relationship—that is, their comfort zone. They are used not only to a specific place and particular routines and habits but also to having the company and skills of another person who takes care of many day-to-day tasks. Being alone feels daunting. These women have to learn who they are in a new environment, often while contending with limited or no resources as well as fear of the unknown.

LIMITATIONS OF A COMFORT ZONE

If we let it, the protective circle of a comfort zone can gradually *establish limits in our life.* A comfort zone is by nature an unchallenging zone; it is a place where we repeat the same routines, interacting with the same people and familiar situations. This means there is no room for tackling new conditions and growing. Unless we choose to expand our comfort zone, we will become more and more comfortable with what we know, and increasingly apprehensive about the unknown.

When we look at comfort zones from this perspective, it is clear there is some risk in being *too* comfortable. We lose opportunities for growth, which requires confronting the unknown, developing resources to deal with unexpected situations, engaging with and adapting to new experiences. If we do not face the new head-on, it will feel more and more threatening, and we will become increasingly fearful and unequipped to deal with new realities. We end up unhappy when we constrain ourselves to what is known, when we avoid situations because of fear, when we diminish our possibilities, and mainly when we then blame ourselves for being in that condition.

So we have to be mindful that, while a comfort zone can be a strength, it can also be a crutch that *creates limitations and a restricted view of our capabilities and options. This leads to unhappiness, along with decreased self-confidence and self-esteem—the drivers for change in life.*

Donna's story provides a firsthand example of some of the pitfalls and challenges that come with an external-source comfort zone and how we can learn to tackle things head-on:

"I met Tony at a concert. We had lunch together the following day, and pretty soon we started dating. I really fell in love with Tony. I liked how masculine he was. His calm attitude, his elegance and optimism were irresistible. I was attracted to him more than I was in love, if that's possible. He fascinated me.

"We eventually married, and our life was terrific; we really enjoyed each other's company. We made plans to buy a house and start a family. I got pregnant when the law company I was an associate at was downsizing, so we decided I'd begin maternity leave early and prepare for our new life with a baby. Soon after, we had baby number two.

"Our life together was changing from being just a couple to having a comfortable, happy family life. We had our kids, our circle of friends, our in-laws. Tony's job was stable. We spent a lot of time outdoors at cookouts, going to parks or the beach. Our relationship was good.

"I don't know when things started changing. I noticed Tony was psychologically absent sometimes. I would say something, and he wouldn't answer. I saw this happening when it was just the two of us. If we were with friends or especially with the in-laws, he was incredibly thoughtful. Our sex life changed too: he would say he was tired. He was very attentive to me for birthdays and holidays. But I knew something was happening.

"I was also changing. I hardly ever thought about my career or working again. Our kids were in elementary school by this point. I organized my life around the kids' activities, school requirements, and summer vacations. My social circle consisted of other moms from the neighborhood and school. Tony and I would still have a beer together every evening in our beautiful little backyard.

"So things seemed fine, but there was something that wasn't going well, and I couldn't put my finger on it. Tony excused himself almost every night from having dinner with us. He said he had urgent emails to answer. I began worrying that he was being dishonest and wondered if he were seeing another woman. He was unpredictable, and I didn't know what to do.

"I started thinking about what it would mean, what I stood to lose if our marriage were in trouble. I loved Tony, and I didn't want our marriage to end. I was afraid about finances. I'd been out of the workforce for quite a few years and felt incapable of returning to my profession. But I also felt stupid for being so afraid of going back to my career.

"On top of my fears about the future, I felt terrible that I couldn't figure out what was going wrong in our relationship. I tried to think that Tony was still okay with me, that there was something else bothering him, and that he would share these concerns with me if I gave him time. *I held on because I needed him to maintain my comfort zone.*

"The more I thought about my inefficiencies, the more fear I felt, and the more I clung to him. I know he sensed this, but his silences and absences were progressively more frequent and unexplained. I didn't want to discover his betrayal. I didn't want even to think that this was a possibility. I felt ashamed that I was too weak to confront him and learn the truth about what was going on. My self-confidence was decreasing steadily.

"I started putting my attention and efforts toward avoiding any problems or negative exchanges with Tony. I felt any small thing could set him off and end our relationship, and I didn't want that. I was unhappy, but my comfort zone was still intact, and that was the only thing that mattered at the time. I was convinced that all women face these types of situations, and that time and patience would resolve things.

"Because I was so afraid of being by myself, so weak and dependent on my comfort zone, Tony started making offensive comments and blaming me when things went poorly. At that point, I wondered what was wrong with him, but more so, *what was wrong with me?* I understood that I needed to change my thinking. That being comfortable because of familiar surroundings *is not the same as being happy.* Yes, we built our comfort zone with love to start, but I had become a slave to it and surrendered my voice in exchange for remaining in this space and keeping things the same.

"Once I realized this, everything started to change. I confronted Tony; we talked and decided to get a divorce. My life afterward was challenging—everything was unfamiliar, but I began with learning to be comfortable with being myself. I made an effort to engage with the realities of daily life around me, which helped me rebuild my confidence. I got a job.

"I developed relationships with other women who were also trying to rebuild their lives and themselves after being slaves to their comfort zones. That was encouraging and positive. These women gave me a different perspective on independence and personal power. Before, what gave me a sense of control was trying to maintain the dependent situation I was in. Reclaiming my freedom brought me tremendous growth, and I started appreciating myself again.

"I have more clarity about what I want from a partner. I want honesty. I want to be respected. I have the right not to be abused verbally. I also learned that when trouble and difficult situations come up, *I don't have to pretend nothing has happened.* Before, I let these things go, but not anymore. I've learned that we live and grow continuously, and it's not healthy to stop at the things we like today. It's not good to be static, period. *Growth comes through change; and we need vision, creativity, and freedom to keep developing.*"

PROBLEMS WITH AN EXTERNAL-SOURCE COMFORT ZONE

If our comfort zone depends on external sources—such as a partner or a husband and his resources—our skills and sense of possibilities erode. The walls of real or perceived limitations grow, and we feel *more and more incapable of stepping out beyond those limits.* If we do not exercise our skills regularly, they become weaker. At the same time, the thought of stepping outside our comfort zone is intimidating, and our fears can increase.

When a person tries to retain the current situation of her comfort zone, even when her circumstances and needs are changing, she becomes *more vulnerable, and her self-esteem declines.* In an unhealthy relationship, the other partner may try to use this to his advantage.

Getting outside of our comfort zone shows us the realities of life, and we become stronger and more efficient because we are putting our abilities into action.

Expectations in an external-source comfort zone

An external-source comfort zone is structured to appeal to women's desires to live up to the expectations society sets for them. The price the woman pays for access to her partner's status, lifestyle, and the sense of security this gives her *is accepting the pressures and demands he makes.* Her comfort zone—that sense of well-being and control—may be threatened if she acts outside of his expectations; she could lose everything. This increases her level of insecurity and fear as well as her dependence on her partner.

These comfort zones are based on a kind of trade: *the more the man provides, the more expectations the woman has to fulfill.* From the perspective of the man, if the woman does not live up to his expectations, she is acting unfairly. If he misbehaves toward her in retaliation, well, he may consider it is *her* fault. A woman in this position assumes a second-place role. Instead of being the protagonist of her life, *she is living according to others' expectations.* A relationship built on this foundation will deteriorate and places the woman at high risk of abuse, whether physical or psychological.

Power dynamics in an external-source comfort zone

The most significant risk a woman faces in this situation is *losing her power* because the condition she must meet to remain in that comfort zone is to submit to his control. In any relational dynamic, *the person with less real or perceived power is at higher risk of becoming insecure and more dependent on his or her partner.* This can often trigger negative aspects of the dominant person's character, and the relationship becomes a harmful, destructive environment in which neither person is right. If we are continually in a submissive role, not using our resources and capabilities, we lose strength, and fear starts getting the upper hand.

Of course, relationships in this type of comfort zone do not always deteriorate to this point. However, even good relationships face these types of challenges every now and then during stressful times, so building awareness is essential.

HOW AN EXTERNAL-SOURCE COMFORT ZONE IS SOCIALIZED

From an early age, girls are taught to prioritize safety, be cautious and careful, get things right, present themselves well, and gain others' approval. Feedback and modeling from parents, family, friends, and teachers instill that this is what is expected of them. Instead of little girls playing to win or for the pleasure of playing, they play to please others and fulfill their expectations.

Parents encourage their daughters to be dependent on others by telling them to be good and nice, so they will find their Prince Charming and all the beautiful things that come with him: house, family, status, independence, respect, and admiration. One of the influences of this type of message is *to link love with economic resources.* A good candidate is someone who is a good provider and can offer his partner security and safety—*a comfort zone.*

In patriarchal societies, a good provider has the right to have certain expectations met in exchange for his resources, and the authority to take action if those conditions are not fulfilled. The requirements for women are to be kind, helpful, and unselfish; never cause trouble, and always prioritize the man's wishes.

It is hard to stand up for ourselves when most of the socialization we get is based on the opposite message—that we should please others and comply with their expectations—especially at a young age when we are reliant on external supports. Besides, many of the role models that young, impressionable minds are exposed also suggest that *being secure and comfortable in the world depends on being a cute girl.*

Later in life, we act according to our partner's expectations and receive the reward of a comfort zone. This means continuing on a predetermined path, a controlled environment where, if we meet societal expectations, we can be assured we are doing everything right—consequently, we will be accepted and maybe even loved. To continue maintaining this comfort zone, we should act according to our partner's expectations. There is no room for exposure to alternative paths or ideas that might create tension.

IN SUMMARY

An external-source comfort zone comes with plenty of opportunities that seem to make life easier, but often leads to frustration because of the limitations it imposes. For example:

- Without the experience of new and challenging situations, there is no progress, learning, or resource-building.
- Dependency decreases freedom, authenticity, and development.
- Along with the woman becoming more dependent and having fewer personal resources, the partner's appreciation and respect often decline; he has to do and provide more, which seems to affirm his thinking that the woman "really can't do or contribute much."

IN CONCLUSION

Women should be critical of accepting and trying to maintain an external-source comfort zone. Our first focus should be on *building our sense of well-being* we can take with us wherever we go, no matter our circumstances or relationship status.

Even in a relationship, we can live in freedom. We can learn that there is excitement in facing challenges, that failure is an opportunity to learn and grow, that the unknown can open to something important. *By going beyond our comfort zone, we grow and become stronger.* We also learn to rise above our fears because the reality is rarely as bad as our thoughts make it out to be.

The secret to success in building a shared comfort zone with a partner is to develop our comfort zone and internal resources *first*, which we can then use as a foundation for when a shared one comes as a possibility into our lives. If a woman has accepted an external-source comfort zone from her partner, and difficult times begin, she will find herself in a tight spot if she does not have resources of her own.

Some of the elements that help to build a personal comfort zone include cultivating personal confidence as well as practical resources, such as a career and savings. Also, staying in touch with life around you so *you can stand on your own two feet.* Ideally, these assets should be built *before* you get attached to an external-source comfort zone. Start as early as you can to develop the skills that enable you to have an autonomous reality and see returns on investment.

If you do not cultivate your own resources—inner strengths and a sense of security, safety, and control—even a relationship with your Prince Charming will be difficult. You will be the weaker partner, and the comfort zone he offers *will come at a price, which may include your independence and dignity.*

It is a law of nature that we are responsible to ourselves before others. Like in an airplane emergency when a person has to put on her oxygen mask before helping others, a *woman's first responsibility is to herself. Healthily building your resources is what will give you security, safety, and confidence, increasing your self-esteem.*

23

Objectification

Objectification[80] is linked to social pressures and the external-source comfort zone (the one provided by a partner or husband). Objectification is when a woman is seen as an object, a "thing" that can be had, given, or acquired, instead of as a whole person. Women have often been seen as sexual objects, to be evaluated by men for their desirability and compliance.[80] In part, society's emphasis on body image for women has developed out of this way of thinking. *The focus on appearance automatically puts a woman's intelligence and competence in second place.* After all, why develop her competencies if she is appreciated primarily for her physical appearance?

Lisa is a student and works part-time as a model to pay her expenses. In her work, appearance is everything, and she puts much effort into meeting the expectations of the firm she models for. Lisa noticed that a lot of her mental energies were going toward thinking about her face, hair, weight, and what she could do or improve to increase her appeal and look sexier. She was unhappy about this because she felt she was treating herself as an object. Moreover, what made her feel even worse was being considered an object by others. *Men's observations about her were related entirely to her body and its appeal.*

Recently, Lisa asked herself: *"What do I want to stand for and represent? This obsession with appearance isn't me."* Lisa is now shifting her mental focus on what is important to her: developing her skills, personal growth, and acting more independently. She recognizes that her body and sexuality are for her to enjoy as she wants, not something for others' control or pleasure.

Many women learn early in life that the way they look is fundamental because appearance can be an avenue to garner attention, resources, and opportunities. For young women navigating the pressures that come from peers to fit in and from parents to find someone to marry, having a perfect body is very much connected to having an ideal life.

However, objectification goes beyond physical appearance. Objectification can happen in any situation in which a woman is not valued for who she is as a person, but for what she can do for a man, what she can bring him. In other words, the point of objectification is, *"What can you do for me?"* rather than, *"Who are you and what is your story?"*

In the upper class or wealthy circles, a man may want a certain type of wife who is particularly beautiful, charming, or submissive, so he can make himself look better and more desirable or boost his social status. The notion of *"trophy wives"* is an example. They are essentially social status symbols, something the man has acquired and enjoys looking at and "having." These relationships are not built on finding a person to love and share life with. They are a *type of exchange*: the man provides the woman with a comfortable life, and in return, she makes him look good. The trophy wife is an "object" to provoke envy in others and show them what a winner the man is. The more beautiful the woman, the more the man has "won."

In the middle or working classes, a man may be looking for *convenience and practicality*, wanting a wife to take care of all domestic and child-rearing duties.

Either way, the woman is valuable so long as *she fulfills the purpose of increasing her partner's value.* This puts enormous pressure on the woman to maintain the standards of domestic life, beauty, or social prestige that the man expects from her for his own, egotistical reasons.

THE CONNECTION BETWEEN OBJECTIFICATION, EXPECTATIONS, AND EXTERNAL-SOURCE COMFORT ZONES

Expectations come with what the man provides the woman he objectifies. For example, she should always look a certain way and maintain a particular weight. She may go through all sorts of plastic surgeries, diets, and beauty treatments—without considering price or risks—to keep the beautiful, thin, youthful appearance he desires. Another condition may be that the woman always comes across as cute and charming, or that she shows submission to her partner and deference to his ability to care for her. Her primary obligations are to look good and answer nicely.

In the woman's mind, someone else is responsible for her life and well-being, *and this is a dangerous place to be.* Adult life is interactive, and things should be equitable in parallel relationships. So it is natural to feel that if someone else is taking care of and providing you with safety and security, you owe him something besides taking second place in the relationship.

This situation may be relaxed and comfortable for the woman, but it also *leaves her powerless.* The authority, decision-making, and resources are all with the man, which creates the sense that it is his right to expect a lot from her. Because he sees her as an object, he considers her something he can control. If he is unhappy with her or she does not fulfill his requirements and requests, the comfortable situation can come to an end. She has to agree with his conditions, satisfy his desires, take second place, and always be mindful of how much she has to lose if she does not comply with his demands.

Among the worst things a woman could do in this context is *to show intelligence, be critical, demonstrate leadership, or gain weight.* With any of the first three, the woman jeopardizes people's impression that the man is the most capable person in the relationship. With the last one, if the woman gains weight, she becomes "less beautiful," and the man's successful image loses points.

In this environment, *men can gradually become controlling and abusive.* However, when this happens, it is frequently the *women who are blamed,* including by their family if its members hold patriarchal views. Women internalize this blame, believing it is their fault, and feel shame. The rationale is: "He treated me so well and took good care of me when I followed his ideas, so of course now there are problems *because I'm repaying his kindness with a bad attitude.* What I need to do is change and show more acceptance and humility."

Women in these situations are often in *denial* about what is happening because confronting the issue may result in the relationship ending. They have been dependent on the man for so long they fear they will not be able to live without him and the resources he provides. Judith's story is an example of this:

Judith, a beautiful, twenty eight year old is married to Ted, a successful entrepreneur ten years older than her. They do not have children and starting a family was never part of their plan. Judith is an only child, and her family placed a lot of importance on personal appearance. From her early teenage years, she was on a never-ending quest to reach a certain level of excellence and beauty that included small plastic surgeries, athletics, and tanning.

When Judith and Ted met five years ago, she was a personal trainer. From the beginning, they had a strong physical attraction to each other and quickly developed a busy social life. Ted liked Judith, but he loved that both men and women stared at her when they appeared in public. Ted was proud of Judith's appearance and became accustomed to her beauty and elegance making him the envy of other men.

Ted was wealthy and told Judith she did not have to work for a living. He would provide whatever she needed. She quit her job and spent a lot of time going to spas and treatments, consulting specialists, and buying products to enhance her appearance. She had a lot of time for this, as Ted traveled often.

Ted was always keen to go to social events when he was in town. But Judith noticed a difference between the way he interacted with her in private and public. He was cutting and mean when they were by themselves, as though she bothered him. But in public, when she looked spectacular, he was doting and attentive.

Slowly, Judith got more and more habituated to the expensive lifestyle that came with being married to Ted. Gradually, she was also losing confidence in her capabilities, although she did not share this with anybody. It was *not fair to complain* when she enjoyed such a luxurious life.

She saw less and less of Ted as the months passed. When he did show up, he would have expensive presents, usually jewelry, and a demand for her to accompany him somewhere. When Judith pushed back on spending so much time and money on herself or voiced disagreement, Ted was verbally abusive. Then Judith put on several pounds. This became a significant source of contention with Ted.

She started realizing the only things that mattered to Ted were her beauty and elegance; *she was not her own person with thoughts and feelings*—maybe she never had been to him—but now she began seeing it. *She was like a beautiful object he had acquired that provoked admiration and respect from other men.* The problem was that Judith was caged in her comfort zone, by this point, and getting out of this situation seemed impossible.

IN CONCLUSION

In all good relationships there is a give-and-take and a sense of equity. Not everything is equal, but there are a fair balance and mutual respect between partners. However, if a man treats a woman as an object, she is a "thing" that belongs to him, which immediately *removes ground for a real relationship.* An object is something to use and to show; it does not have any power and is at the complete disposal of the owner.

In the case of an objectified woman, she has usually been selected based on appearance. Since looks are all that matter, every effort goes toward improving and maintaining her beauty. No consideration is given to developing her skills, learning, growing, having a purpose, or contributing to the world around her. Her sole goal is to please the man, who is the provider and has all the rights. This becomes a *relationship between the powerful and the submissive.*

The foundation for a healthy union starts with *two independent people taking mutual responsibility for their relationship and working together to create balance and opportunities for growth.*

24

Benevolent Sexism

One evening, my daughter and I took in an excellent country music show by our friend Clay. Afterward, we were standing outside the venue when a lady approached us, followed by her husband. She commented on how fun the show was and asked if we were mother and daughter. She was smiling happily. The husband made a gesture indicating that she was drunk, asked us to "please excuse her," and they left.

Later I thought: Why wasn't she free to say whatever she wanted? Why did he treat her like a minor who had done something wrong? Of course, we expect an adult coming out of a bar to have had a few drinks and perhaps be more chatty than usual. It was not as though she had been rude.

To me, this was an example of *benevolent sexism*: the husband taking care of his "weak" wife, whose behavior he considers inappropriate. It may look like what he does is for her good, to help her, but in reality this is about *displaying power*. Even if it is *unintentional*, he is acting *following traditional gender roles*, in which men determine what conditions or behaviors are appropriate for women.

Benevolent sexism is a concept introduced by Glick and Fiske [81,82,83] that highlights that some forms of sexism seem "positive," because they result in a protective attitude toward women—the desire to start a relationship with a woman and to care for her in a paternalistic sense. By contrast, hostile sexism is clearly harmful—the desire to dominate a woman, to denigrate and own her. *Benevolent sexism is nonetheless still sexist and very much related to the external-source comfort zone.*

When a woman fulfills or exceeds society's expectations, others around her take notice, and she is rewarded and respected. As part of this, she is perceived as an ideal candidate for a long-term partnership or marriage, which comes with the promise of a sense of protection, a roof over her head, someone to care for her, financial support, security, and safety. This sounds good if you do not consider this type of "protection" a barrier to personal growth and freedom. In part, the man's affection stems from the sense that the woman needs the safety and security he offers because she is inferior in some way. *She does not have the knowledge, the strength, or the skills to take care of herself in the big bad world,* so she needs him, which appeals to masculine pride.

Implicit in benevolent sexism is that women are not exposed to "challenging" work situations that go beyond known circumstances (for example, the family business) or that are in fields considered inappropriate for women. In other words, women are useful in family environments and "gender-appropriate" careers but generally "lack competence" to deal with the outside world. This limits their opportunity to exercise creativity, learn by trial and error, and try new things. Instead, a woman's efforts are concentrated on repeating well-known chores correctly, as part of showing gratitude for all the support, protection, care, and warmth she receives—her little comfort zone.

Benevolent sexism is insidious, pervasive, and subtle,[84] even though it does not seem as bad as hostile or blatant sexism. However, it still can be detrimental because it maintains *the traditional gender roles.*[85] Women feel comfortable and have a sense of control in their comfort zone, *leading to a lack of action and progress.*

In a relationship, benevolent sexism *limits the woman's options and increases the man's power.* Women might not complain, or feel they have no right to, if their partner is perceived as affectionate, considerate, and generous.[86] They do not want to upset the current situation and risk losing their comfort zone, so it is better not to acknowledge what they do not like. Plus, everyone approves of them for behaving like a good woman and not interfering in a man's (superior) world, per traditional gender roles.

Benevolent sexism is connected with women's perceived *lack of self-sufficiency,* so it provokes a decrease in women's self-esteem and self-confidence. *As the woman's self-esteem weakens, her level of dependency grows.* Over time, women in this situation come to depend on their partners to the point that they feel incapable of leading an independent life. On the other hand, the woman's growing dependency on the man encourages in him a broader sense of responsibility to provide and protect as well as to control their environment. Through this, *her external-source comfort zone is strengthened.*

I have talked with women in their forties and fifties whose children were in their late teens, and many of them were unable to even think about holding a job, starting a career, or living an otherwise independent life because of the *disastrous effects of benevolent sexism on their self-esteem.* These women feel that they do not have control of their own lives, but do not know how to change things. Many women in this situation face the challenge of standing up to temptations, such as excessive shopping or drinking, which provide short-term, temporary relief from feeling out of control.

Katie, one of my clients, was in this situation. From the outside, everything in her life looked good. Her husband had a prosperous business, her kids were studious and well-behaved, and she always had suggestions for the latest wellness treatment, cosmetic procedure, or a trendy brand. Her family of origin was traditional and strict, and she got married right out of college. She has never had a job, and her diploma was another piece of décor in the house.

The essential part of her life was caring for her husband and kids. Yet Katie's children were soon off to university, and she was coming to the empty nest stage of life. Everybody in her home was going to be independent and have clear objectives except Katie. Her general approach to difficult situations was to spend money; she invested in *retail therapy* almost daily.

Katie and I talked about the challenges she would face if she did not step outside her comfort zone and put herself into new situations, even though it would be hard at first. If she tried to maintain the status quo, she would likely become more dependent on her husband, creating stress in their relationship. Having an uncertain future was scary for Katie, but she was determined to find something new she could do for herself that would give her a sense of purpose.

We discussed *how our identity is informed by our growth*—the journey we undertake to reach a new stage or goal in life. If we see no future for ourselves beyond maintaining the daily routines and have nothing to look forward to, *we will find ourselves in big trouble.*

WHY BENEVOLENT SEXISM IS SO STRONG

Benevolent sexism is strong because it is *subtle*. It is not always visible or happening out in the open, in contrast with hostile sexism, which is much more evident. Most people these days know that hostile sexism is rude and something to avoid.

Benevolent sexism often looks good on the surface—like *honorable actions or genuine help to resolve a problem*, rather than repressive or oppressive behavior. It also creates a situation in which *both parties seem to gain something:* the man maintains his privileged position of superiority and authority, and the woman gains access to a comfort zone based on the man's resources, power, and prestige.

Benevolent sexism is linked to the *concept of power*, a fundamental component of masculinity, which holds that a man needs to show control related to himself and his context. He does this by establishing a relationship that sets up a way of helping (providing and protecting) that makes him look good. However, it also creates dependency.

The human attraction has developed over generations in connection with *biological survival*. Inherently, it results in men being attracted to women with certain physical traits and psychological qualities typically associated with femininity, and women being attracted to men who have strength, power, resources, and other attributes usually associated with masculinity .[87] However, we have also evolved our knowledge of *what is healthy for human identity and personal growth*, and it is possible for both parties in a relationship to develop a fulfilling connection that nurtures their partnership *without compromising the autonomy of either side.*

WHY WOMEN ACCEPT A SUBMISSIVE ROLE

Socialization of gender stereotypes underlies the reason women take a submissive role, such as, the idea that a woman should seek out a reliable, masculine partner because he will be able to defend her and provide for her, which will increase her value. Why wouldn't a woman pick Prince Charming—a perfect illustration of masculinity—and the road to happily-ever-after over a man who is perceived as weak, emotional, or cowardly? Masculinity implies control and authority, including in relationships with women. Men's dominance over women is a crucial feature of traditional masculinity, which is accepted by many women as *taking care of and protecting them.*

Another thing women are taught is that if they present themselves as *a complement, rather than competition,* to a man and his resources, they will have a better chance of establishing a relationship with him. Importantly, part of gender-specific expectations for women is that being a good woman means taking a second-place role and following versus leading, responding to domination with docility and obedience. A woman taking control or a position of authority goes against expectations and might lead to negative consequences, that are seen as "justified" because the woman went against the stereotype.

HOW BENEVOLENT SEXISM DEVELOPS

Benevolent sexism develops when traditional gender roles are upheld, and there is a power imbalance between boys/men and girls/women. Men hold the decision-making power, and women should behave in a certain way to feel validated. Girls hear that being feminine means being kind, well-behaved, obedient, agreeable, and humble (not too confident or self-assured). To be a good girl and then a good woman means complying with social norms that establish how we have to be and what we can do.

While progress has been made in many parts of the world to advance women's rights, women in conservative, religious, rural, and minority ethnic groups are still subject to many social pressures. A girl growing up in these environments is likely to hear that if she does not behave, no man will be interested in her. *This puts a ceiling on how women think about their own life and future.* If you have never heard that something is possible, it is difficult to conceive of yourself doing that thing.

Family pressure may support the idea that life without a man (and a family) is undesirable and is, in fact, a type of failure. To avoid this, girls and women *follow the path of femininity laid out for them.*

CONSEQUENCES OF BENEVOLENT SEXISM

Benevolent sexism appears attractive to both men and women. As I already mentioned, for men, it is a way to maintain paternalism and increase their sense of masculinity. For women, it is a road to access the benefits of a man's protection, care, and the comfort zone he provides.

However, benevolent sexism has *negative consequences* for both parties. Men are constricted by the requirements and restrictions of masculinity, including not expressing emotions, always being reliable and resilient, never showing uncertainty or asking for help. Women suffer the limitations that come from not having autonomy and the fear of losing their comfort zone if they do not follow traditional gender roles.

In my clinical practice, I saw that *relationships based on benevolent sexism deteriorate over time.* As the appeal of the early stages of a relationship fades, the man starts treating his partner with less respect or affection. She feels more vulnerable and insecure in the relationship, which increases her dependency on him and, in turn, provokes his irritation, frustration, and sometimes anger toward her. As a woman's lack of autonomy reduces her resources, she usually becomes more dependent and submissive, less creative and resilient, and her self-confidence gradually fades. Stephanie and John's story is one example:

Stephanie and John had reached an impasse in their marriage. Stephanie had always put John and his opinions, desires, and plans first. She was a housewife with a part-time job and apparently liked this arrangement. She was a modest woman, always lovely, with a kind word and generosity for everyone.

Behind closed doors, however, John was an abusive partner, and Stephanie was submissive to him. John had become exasperated with Stephanie's constant niceness; he said he wanted something "real" from her and started verbally abusing her to goad her into a "genuine" response. Stephanie did not know what to do and often burst into tears; John would tell her what a weak woman she was. Stephanie wanted to turn things around and recover her sense of self-worth, but she knew it would be an uphill struggle: *depending on John and thinking of herself as unimportant and weak had become her second nature.*

IN CONCLUSION

The problem with benevolent sexism is that, while it might appear gallant, courteous, and helpful, it does not promote women's development. In fact, it does just the opposite: it increases dependency. Moreover, because the "chivalrous help" is not rooted in an egalitarian relationship between men and women, it *keeps traditional gender roles alive.*

Women put aside their wishes and autonomy; they behave nicely and assume second place—as less intelligent, less talented, and less capable than men—in exchange for being in a relationship under a man's protection and the comfort zone he provides.

Both the cons and apparent pros of benevolent sexism *maintain and increase gender inequality* because the rewards look attractive, and the differences between genders are seen as inherent and impossible to change.

25

Looking Forward

Dear reader, across this journey, I have talked about the many ways we women face intense social pressures that can limit our lives. I want to close by telling you *it is within your power to change this situation.*

The first step to making any change is to understand what we are up against. In this case, it means having an objective view of the challenges that women across societies and generations have faced time and again. When we understand what is at the root of the problem, we are prepared to invoke change.

That is the purpose of this book: to help you realize it is not okay to resign your life to pleasing others in exchange for comfort. We should find the freedom, bravery, and courage we need—and put in the work—to cultivate the resources required to create our own life: the one we want, that takes into account our desires, needs, and talents.

We need to consolidate our power by disregarding and rising above the pressures and expectations I described in part one of this book. We can say goodbye to fear and envy of other women's successes because we too can develop and strive for our own goals and greatness. We need to realize the subtle power of benevolent sexism and support each other in cultivating our strength and self-confidence to stand up for who we are. We should see that relying on external-source comfort zones can limit our possibilities and weaken our self-esteem. We must practice resilience when confronted by shame and guilt, the harmful residue of patriarchal ideology. Above all, remember that we are unique individuals with unlimited possibilites, not objects for the gratification and service of others.

I hope the information in this book empowers you to look at yourself and the world around you with new eyes. To understand that there are longstanding systems, such as patriarchy and sexism, that have obstructed women's freedom of self-determination and caused deep unhappiness and frustration, not to mention embarrassment from feeling that these problematic situations were our fault. To know that you do not have to live this way.

Look ahead to the doors of change that are open to you, and for the ways you can be a role model of autonomy and self-confidence. Together, we can build a new future. As women, we can and should support each other in developing resilience and being agents of change. We can be the positive wave that causes all boats to rise.

As I arrive at the close of this book, I have also reached the end of a long and productive journey that has taught and transformed me. Thank you for being with me until this last page.

If this book has caused you to feel surprised, challenged, or even uncomfortable at points, then I have done my job. What I have written about has happened to women of all ages and cultures around the world. Many of us had spent at least some of our lives aiming to please others, trying to be and do what others want, and feeling bad and selfish when we thought we fell short. We have had moments of being scared of our successes, worried about gossip, and of questioning our self-worth.

I close here with an invitation to you to return to yourself, to your unique identity, to your unspoken hopes and desires. *From this most profound part of yourself, start building your life with creativity, freedom, responsibility, appreciation, and gratitude for having a present and a future that belong entirely to you!* And from this full heart, *let's give the world the good that is in us—the brilliance, strength, skills, and understanding that each of us possesses—in an equitable and mutual exchange.*

ENDNOTES
References and Bibliography

Sources cited in text and resources
used to generate thoughts about the subjects

Disclaimer: I reviewed pertinent literature and research on the topic. However, most of the time, the conclusions are based on my personal and professional experience.

1. Bandura, A. (1989). Self-regulation of motivation and action through internal standards and goal systems. In L. A. Pervin (Ed.), *Goal concepts in personality and social psychology* (pp. 19–85). Hillsdale, NJ: Lawrence Erlbaum Associates, Inc.

Bem, S. L. (1974). The measurement of psychological androgyny. *Journal of Consulting and Clinical Psychology, 42*, 155–162. doi:10.1037/h0036215

Berdahl, J. L. (2007). The sexual harassment of uppity women. *Journal of Applied Psychology, 92*, 425–437. doi:10.1037/0021-9010.92.2.425

Burgess, D., & Borgida, E. (1999). Who women are, who women should be: Descriptive and prescriptive gender stereotyping in sex discrimination. *Psychology, Public Policy, and Law, 5*, 665–692. doi:10.1037/1076-8971.5.3.665
Dall'Ara, E., & Maass, A. (1999). Studying sexual harassment in the laboratory: Are egalitarian women at higher risk? *Sex Roles, 41*, 681–704. doi:10.1023/A:1018816025988

Fiske, S. T. (1993). Controlling other people: The impact of power on stereotyping. *American Psychologist, 48*(6), 621–628. doi:10.1037/0003-066X.48.6.621

Fiske, S. T., Cuddy, A. J. C., Glick, P., & Xu, J. (2002). A model of (often mixed) stereotype content: Competence and warmth respectively follow from perceived status and competition. *Journal of Personality and Social Psychology, 82,* 878–902. doi:10.1037/0022-3514.82.6.878

Fiske, S. T., & Stevens, L. E. (1993). What's so special about sex? Gender stereotyping and discrimination. In S. Oskamp & M. Costanzo (Eds.), *Gender issues in contemporary society* (pp. 173–196). Thousand Oaks, CA: Sage Publications.

Fiske, S. T., Xu, J., Cuddy, A. C., & Glick, P. (1999). (Dis)respecting versus (dis)liking: Status and interdependence predict ambivalent stereotypes of competence and warmth. *Journal of Social Issues, 55,* 473–489.

Gill, M. J. (2004). When information does not deter stereotyping: Prescriptive stereotyping can bias judgments under conditions that discourage descriptive stereotyping. *Journal of Experimental Social Psychology, 40,* 619–632. doi:10.1016/j.jesp.2003.12.001

Glick, P., & Fiske, S. T. (1999). Sexism and other "isms": Independence, status, and the ambivalent content of stereotypes. In W. B. Swann, J. H. Langlois, & L. A. Gilbert (Eds.), *Sexism and stereotypes in modern society: The gender science of Janet Taylor Spence* (pp. 193–221). Washington, DC: American Psychological Association. doi:10.1037/10277-008

Hays, P. (2001). *Addressing cultural complexities in practice.* Washington, DC: American Psychological Association.

Heilman, M. E. (2001). Description and prescription: How gender stereo-types prevent women's ascent up the organizational ladder. *Journal of Social Issues, 57,* 657–674. doi:10.1111/0022-4537.00234

Heilman, M. E., & Okimoto, T. G. (2007). Why are women penalized for success at male tasks? The implied communality deficit. *Journal of Applied Psychology, 92,* 81–92. doi:10.1037/0021-9010.92.1.81

Heilman, M. E., Wallen, A. S., Fuchs, D., & Tamkins, M. M. (2004). Penalties for success: Reactions to women who succeed at male gender-typed tasks. *Journal of Applied Psychology, 89,* 416–427. doi:10.1037/0021-9010.89.3.416

Hofstede, G., & Bond, M. H. (1988). *The Confucius connection: From cultural roots to economic growth.* Organizational Dynamics, *16,* 5–21. doi:10.1016/0090-2616(88)90009-5

Maass, A., Cadinu, M., Guarnieri, G., & Grasselli, A. (2003). Sexual harassment under social identity threat: The computer harassment par-adigm. *Journal of Personality and Social Psychology, 85,* 853–870. doi:10.1037/0022-3514.85.5.853

Markus, H. R., & Kitayama, S. (1991). Culture and the self: Implications for cognition, emotion, and motivation. *Psychological Review, 98,* 224–253. doi:10.1037/0033-295X.98.2.224

Phelan, J. E., & Rudman, L. A. (2010). Reactions to ethnic deviance: The role of backlash in racial stereotype maintenance. *Journal of Personality and Social Psychology, 99,* 265–281. doi:10.1037/a0018304

Prentice, D. A., & Carranza, E. (2002). What women and men should be, shouldn't be, are allowed to be, and don't have to be: The contents of prescriptive gender stereotypes. *Psychology of Women Quarterly, 26,* 269–281. doi:10.1111/1471-6402.t01-1-00066

Rudman, L. A. (1998). Self-promotion as a risk factor for women: The costs and benefits of counterstereotypical impression management. *Journal of Personality and Social Psychology, 74,* 629–645. doi:10.1037/0022-3514.74.3.629

Rudman, L. A., & Glick, P. (1999). Feminized management and backlash toward agentic women: The hidden costs to women of a kinder, gentler image of middle managers. *Journal of Personality and Social Psychology, 77,* 1004–1010. doi:10.1037/0022-3514.77.5.1004

Rudman, L. A., & Glick, P. (2001). Prescriptive gender stereotypes and backlash toward agentic women. *Journal of Social Issues, 57,* 743–762. doi:10.1111/0022-4537.00239

2. Eagly, A. H., & Wood, W. (1999). The origins of sex differences in human behavior: Evolved dispositions versus social roles. *American Psychologist, 54*(6), 408–423. Retrieved from http://dx.doi.org/10.1037/0003-066X.54.6.408

3. Fiske, S. T., Bersoff, D. N., Borgida, E., Deaux, K., & Heilman, M. E. (1991). Social science research on trial: Use of sex stereotyping research in Price Waterhouse v. Hopkins. *American Psychologist, 46*(10), 1049–1060.

4. Rudman, L. A., & Glick, P. (1999). Feminized management and backlash toward agentic women: The hidden costs to women of a kinder, gentler image of middle managers. *Journal of Personality and Social Psychology, 77*(5), 1004–1010. Retrieved from http://dx.doi.org/10.1037/0022-3514.77.5.1004

5. Frederickson, B. L., & Roberts, T. (1997). Objectification theory: Toward understanding women's lived experience and mental health risks.

Psychology of Women Quarterly, 21(2),173–206. Retrieved from https://doi.org/10.1111/j.1471-6402.1997.tb00108.x

6. Miller, R. (2011). *Intimate relationships* (6th ed.). New York, NY: McGraw-Hill Education.

7. Lorenzo, G. L., Biesanz, J. C., & Human, L. J. (2010). What is beautiful is good and more accurately understood: Physical attractiveness and accuracy in first impressions of personality. *Psychological Science, 21*(12), 1777–1782.

8. Frederickson, B. L., & Roberts, T. (1997). Objectification theory: Toward understanding women's lived experience and mental health risks. *Psychology of Women Quarterly, 21*(2),173–206. Retrieved from https://doi.org/10.1111/j.1471-6402.1997.tb00108.x

9. Asch, S. E. (1946). Forming impressions of personality. *Journal of Abnormal and Social Psychology, 41*, 1230–1240.

10. Willis, J., & Todorov, A. (2006). First impressions: Making up your mind after a 100-ms exposure to a face. *Psychological Science, 17*(7), 592–598. Retrieved from www.jstor.org/stable/40064417

11. Flett, G. L., & Hewitt, P. L. (2002). Perfectionism and maladjustment: An overview of theoretical, directional, and treatment issues. In G. L. Flett & P. L. Hewitt (Eds.), *Perfectionism: Theory, research, and treatment* (No. 7; pp. 5–31). Washington, DC: American Psychological Association.

12. Lytton, H., & Romney, D. M. (1991). Parents' differential socialization of boys and girls: A meta-analysis. *Psychological Bulletin, 109*(2), 267–296.

Wüstenberg, S., Greiff, S., Molnár, G., Funke, J. (2014, January). Cross-national gender differences in complex problem solving and their determinants. *Learning and Individual Differences, 29,*18–29.

13. Tangney, J. P., & Dearing, R. L. (2002). *Shame and guilt.* New York, NY: Guilford Press.

14. Strube, M. (1988). The decision to leave an abusive relationship: Empirical evidence and theoretical issues. *Psychological Bulletin, 104*(2), 236–250.

Katz, J., Tirone, V., Schukrafft, M. (2012). Breaking up is hard to do: psychological entrapment and women's commitment to violent dating relationships. *Violence and Victims, 27*(4):455–69.

15. Hibbs, C. (2014). Patriarchy. In T. Teo (Ed.), *Encyclopedia of critical psychology.* New York, NY: Springer.

16. Traister, R. (2016). *All the single ladies.* New York, NY: Simon & Schuster.

17. Parker K., & Stepler, R. (2017, September14). As U.S. marriage rate hovers at 50%, education gap in marital status widens. Pew Research Center. Retrieved from http://www.pewresearch.org/fact-tank/2017/09/14/as-u-s-marriage-ratehovers-at-50-education-gap-in-marital-status-widens/

18. United Nations Children's Fund. (2018). *Child marriage.* Retrieved from https://data.unicef.org/topic/child-protection/child-marriage/

19. Hibbs, C. (2014). Patriarchy. In T. Teo (Ed.), *Encyclopedia of critical psychology.* New York, NY: Springer.

O'Reilly, A. (Ed.). (2010). *Encyclopedia of motherhood, Vol. 1.* Thousand Oaks, CA: SAGE Publications.

20. Sharp, E. A., & Ganong, L. (2011). "I'm a loser, I'm not married, let's just all look at me": Ever-single women's perceptions of their social environment. *Journal of Family Issues, 32*(7), 956–980. Retrieved from http://dx.doi.org/10.1177/0192513X10392537

21. Buunk, A. P., Park, J. H., & Duncan, L. A. (2010). Cultural variation in parental influence on mate choice. *Cross-Cultural Research, 44*(1), 23–40.

22. Tangney, J. P., & Dearing, R. L. (2002). *Shame and guilt.* New York, NY: Guilford Press.

23. O'Brien, J. (2015). Heterosexism and homophobia. In J. D. Wright (Ed.), *International encyclopedia of the social and behavioral sciences* (2nd ed.), 790–795. Retrieved from https://doi.org/10.1016/B978-0-08-097086-8.10204-1

24. Hetrick, E. S., & Martin, A. D. (1987). Developmental issues and their resolution for gay and lesbian adolescents. *Journal of Homosexuality, 14*(1–2 Spring), 25–43.

25. Bayer, R. (1981). *Homosexuality and American psychiatry: The politics of diagnosis.* New York, NY: Basic Books.

26. Drescher, J., & Zucker, K. J. (Eds.). (2006). *Ex-gay research: Analyzing the Spitzer study and its relation to science, religion, politics, and culture.* New York: Harrington Park Press.

Morrow, S. L., & Beckstead, A. L. (2004). Conversion therapies for same-sex attracted clients in religious conflict: Context, predisposing factors, experiences, and implications for therapy. *The Counseling Psychologist, 32,* 641–650.

27. Friedman, C., & Leaper, C. (2010). Sexual-minority college women's experiences with discrimination: Relations with identity and collective action. *Psychology of Women Quarterly, 34*(2), 152–164. doi:10.1111/j.1471-6402.2010.01558.x

Szymanski, D. M. (2004). Relations among dimensions of feminism and internalized heterosexism in lesbians and bisexual women. *Sex Roles, 51,* 145–159. doi:10.1023/B: SERS.0000037759. 33014.55

28. World Economic Forum (2017). What you need to know about LGBT rights in 11 maps. Retrieved from https://www.weforum.org/agenda/2017/03/what-you-need-to-know-about-lgbt-rights-in-11-maps/

29. Mink, M. D., Lindley, L. L., & Weinstein, A. A. (2014). Stress, stigma, and sexual minority status: The intersectional ecology model of LGBTQ health. *Journal of Gay & Lesbian Social Services, 26*(4), 502–521. doi: 10.1080/10538720.2014.953660

30. Tangney, J. P., & Dearing, R. L. (2002). *Shame and guilt.* New York, NY: Guilford Press.

31. Lewis, R. J., Padilla, M. A., Milletich, R. J., Kelley, M. L., Winstead, B. A., Lau-Barraco, C., & Mason, T. B. (2015). Emotional distress, alcohol use, and bidirectional partner violence among lesbian women. *Violence Against Women, 21*(8), 917–938.

32. Kertzner, R. M., Meyer, I. H., Frost, D. M., & Stirratt, M. J. (2009). Social and psychological well-being in lesbians, gay men, and bisexuals: The effect of race, gender, age, and sexual identity. *American Journal of Orthopsychiatry, 79*(4), 500–510.

33. D'Augelli, A. R., & Hart, M. (1987). Gay women, men, and families in rural settings: Toward the development of helping communities. *American Journal of Community Psychology, 15*(1), 79–93.

34. University of California, Santa Barbara. (2018). Homosexuality and religion. Retrieved from http://www.soc.ucsb.edu/sexinfo/article/homosexuality-and-religion

35. Flammer, L. J. (2001). The nature of prejudice: Dimensions and patterns of racism, sexism, classism, and heterosexism among social groups. *Dissertation Abstracts International: Section B: The Sciences and Engineering, 62*(5-B), 2534.

36. Pew Research Center. (2017, October 5). *The partisan divide on political values grows even wider: Homosexuality, gender, and religion.* Retrieved from http://www.people-press.org/2017/10/05/5-homosexuality-gender-and-religion/

37. Armenia, A., & Troia, B. (2017). Evolving opinions: Evidence on marriage equality attitudes from panel data. *Social Science Quarterly, 98*(1), 185–195.

    Pew Research Center. (2017, June 26). *Changing attitudes on gay marriage.* Retrieved from http://www.pewforum.org/fact-sheet/changing-attitudes-on-gay-marriage/

38. Slaughter, A. (2012, July/August). Why women still can't have it all. *The Atlantic.* Retrieved from https://www.theatlantic.com/magazine/archive/2012/07/why-women-still-cant-have-it-all/309020/

39. Fitzgerald, L. F., Drasgow, F., Hulin, C. L., Gelfand, M. J., & Magley, V. J. (1997). Antecedents and consequences of sexual harassment in organizations: A test of an integrated model. *Journal of Applied Psychology, 82*(4), 579–589.

40. National Women's Law Center. (2016). *Workplace justice: Frequently asked questions about sexual harassment in the workplace.* Retrieved from https://nwlc-ciw49tixgw5lbab.stackpathdns.com/wp-content/uploads/2016/11/Sexual-Harassment-FAQ.pdf

41. Siegel, R. B. (2004). Introduction. In C. A. MacKinnon and R. B. Siegel (Eds.), *Directions in sexual harassment law* (pp. 1–40). New Haven, CT: Yale University Press.

42. U.S. Equal Employment Opportunity Commission. (2016). *Select task force on the study of harassment in the workplace* (p. 8). Retrieved from https://www.eeoc.gov/eeoc/task_force/harassment/upload/report.pdf

43. Lagerberg, F. (2016, March 8). Women in business: Turning promise into practice. Retrieved from https://www.grantthornton.global/en/insights/articles/women-in-business-2016/

44. Slaughter, A. (2012, July/August). Why women still can't have it all. *The Atlantic*. Retrieved from https://www.theatlantic.com/magazine/archive/2012/07/why-women-still-cant-have-it-all/309020/

45. Griffin, G. (2017). *A dictionary of gender studies*. New York, NY: Oxford University Press.

46. Laughlin, K. (2011). Introduction. In K. Laughlin & J. Castledine (Eds.), *Breaking the wave: Women, their organizations, and feminism, 1945-1985* (pp. 1–8). New York: Routledge.

47. Swirsky, J. M., & Angelone, D. J. (2016). Equality, empowerment, and choice: what does feminism mean to contemporary women? *Journal of Gender Studies, 25*(4), 445–460. doi: 10.1080/09589236.2015.1008429

48. Singh, A., & Misra, N. (2009). Loneliness, depression, and sociability in old age. *Industrial Psychology Journal, 18*(1), 51–55. doi: 10.4103/0972-6748.57861

49. Frejka, T. (2017). Childlessness in the United States. In M. Kreyenfeld & D. Konietzka (Eds.), *Childlessness in Europe: Contexts, causes, and consequences.*

Demographic Research Monographs (A series of the Max Planck Institute for Demographic Research). Cham, Switzerland: Springer. Retrieved from https://link.springer.com/chapter/10.1007/978-3-319-44667-7_8#Tab2

50. Matthews, R., & Matthews, A. M. (1986). Infertility and involuntary childlessness: The transition to nonparenthood. *Journal of Marriage and Family, 48*(3), 641–649.

51. Hargrove, D. S. (1986). Ethical issues in rural mental health practice. *Professional Psychology: Research and Practice, 17*(1), 20–23. Retrieved from http://dx.doi.org/10.1037/0735-7028.17.1.20

52. Stockman, A. F. (1990). Dual relationships in rural mental health practice: An ethical dilemma. *Journal of Rural Community Psychology, 11*(2), 31–45.

53. Cook, A. D., Copans, S. A., & Schetky, D. H. (1998). Psychiatric treatment of children and adolescents in rural communities: Myths and realities. *Child and Adolescent Psychiatric Clinics of North America, 7*(3), 673–690.

54. Campbell, C. D., Gordon, M. C., & Chandler, A. A. (2002). Wide open spaces: Meeting mental health needs in underserved rural areas. *Journal of Psychology and Christianity, 21*(4), 325–332.

55. Wagenfeld, M. O. (2003). A snapshot of rural and frontier America. In B. H. Stamm (Ed.), *Rural behavioral health care: An interdisciplinary guide* (p. 37). Washington, DC: American Psychological Association. Retrieved from http://dx.doi.org/10.1037/10489-002

56. Mulder, P. L., Shellenberger, S., Striegel, R., Jumper-Thurman, P., Danda, C. E., Kenkel, M. B.,... & Hager, A. (2000). The behavioral health care needs of rural women. Retrieved from https://www.apa.org/practice/programs/rural/rural-women.pdf

57. Cromartie, J. (2017). Rural areas show overall population decline and shifting regional patterns of population change. USDA Economic Research Service. Retrieved from https://www.ers.usda.gov/amber-waves/2017/september/rural-areas-show-overall-population-decline-and-shifting-regional-patterns-of-population-change/

58. Wilson, S., Peterson, G., & Wilson, P. (1993). The process of educational and occupational attainment of adolescent females from low-income, rural families. *Journal of Marriage and Family, 55*(1), 158–175. doi:10.2307/352966

59. National Rural Health Association. (2013). *Rural women's health*. Retrieved from https://www.ruralhealthweb.org/getattachment/Advocate/Policy-Documents/RuralWomensHealth-(1).pdf.aspx

American Psychological Association. (n.d.). *APA report: Executive summary of the behavioral health care needs of rural women*. Retrieved from https://www.apa.org/pubs/info/reports/rural-women-summary.pdf

60. Myers, J. E., & Gill, C. G. (2004). Poor, rural, and female: Understudied, under-counseled, more at-risk. *Journal of Mental Health Counseling, 26*, 225–242.

61. Myers, J. E. (2003). Coping with caregiving stress: A wellness-oriented, strengths-based approach for family counselors. *The Family Journal, 11*, 1–9.

62. Hayslip, B., & Patrick, J. (2003). Working with custodial grandparents. New York, NY: Springer.

63. *Wendt, S., & Cheers, B. (2002). Impacts of rural culture on domestic violence. Rural Social Work, 7(1), 22–32.*

64. Mitchell, R. E., and Hodson, C. A. (1983), Coping with domestic violence: Social support and psychological health among battered women. *American Journal of Community Psychology, 11*, 629–654. doi:10.1007/BF0089660

65. National Rural Health Association. (2013). *Rural women's health.* Retrieved from https://www.ruralhealthweb.org/getattachment/Advocate/Policy-Documents/RuralWomensHealth-(1).pdf.aspx

American Psychological Association. (n.d.). *APA report: Executive summary of the behavioral health care needs of rural women.* Retrieved from https://www.apa.org/pubs/info/reports/rural-women-summary.pdf

66. World Health Organization. (2018). *Gender and women's mental health.* Retrieved from http://www.who.int/mental_health/prevention/genderwomen/en/

67. Jameson, J. P., & Blank, M. B. (2007). The role of clinical psychology in rural mental health services: Defining problems and developing solutions. *Clinical Psychology: Science and Practice, 14*(3), 283–298.

68. Michalski, J. H. (2004). Making sociological sense out of trends in intimate partner violence: The social structure of violence against women. *Violence Against Women, 10*(6), 652–675. doi: 10.1177/1077801204265018

69. Pew Research Center. (2018). *Religious landscape study.* Retrieved from http://www.pewforum.org/religious-landscape-study/

70. Kurdek, L. (1998). Relationship outcomes and their predictors: Longitudinal evidence from heterosexual married, gay cohabiting, and lesbian cohabiting couples. *Journal of Marriage and Family, 60*(3), 553–568.

71. Peplau, L. A., & Fingerhut, A. W. (2007). The close relationships of lesbians and gay men. *Annual Review of Psychology, 58*(1), 405–424.

72. Perales, F., & Baxter, J. (2017). Sexual identity and relationship quality in Australia and the United Kingdom. *Family Relations, 67,* 55–69. doi:10.1111/fare.12293

73. Schneider, S. K., O'Donnell, L., Stueve, A., & Coulter, R. W. S. (2012). Cyberbullying, school bullying, and psychological distress: A regional census of high school students. *American Journal of Public Health, 102*(1), 171–177.

74. Platt, L.F., & Lenzen, A.L. (2013). Sexual orientation microaggressions and the experience of sexual minorities. *Journal of Homosexuality, 60*(7), 1011–1034. doi: 10.1080/00918369.2013.774878

75. Asch, S. E. (1946). Forming impressions of personality. *Journal of Abnormal and Social Psychology, 41,* 1230–1240.

76. Lorenzo, G. L., Biesanz, J. C., & Human, L. J. (2010). What is beautiful is good and more accurately understood: Physical attractiveness and accuracy in first impressions of personality. *Psychological Science, 21*(12), 1777–1782.

Willis, J., & Todorov, A. (2006). First impressions: Making up your mind after a 100-ms exposure to a face. *Psychological Science, 17*(7), 592–598. Retrieved from www.jstor.org/stable/40064417

77. Tangney, J. P., & Dearing, R. L. (2002). *Shame and guilt.* New York, NY: Guilford Press.

78. Maslow, A. (1943). A theory of human motivation. *Psychological Review, 50,* 370–396.

79. Seligman, M. E. P. (1972). Learned helplessness. *Annual Review of Medicine, 23*, 407–412.

80. Frederickson B. L., & Roberts, T. (1997). Objectification theory: Toward understanding women's lived experience and mental health risks. *Psychology of Women Quarterly, 21*(2),173–206. Retrieved from https://doi.org/10.1111/j.1471-6402.1997.tb00108.x

81. Glick, P., & Fiske, S. (1996). The ambivalent sexism inventory: Differentiating hostile and benevolent sexism. *Journal of Personality and Social Psychology, 70*, 491–512.

82. Glick, P., & Fiske, S. (1999). The ambivalence toward men inventory: Differentiating hostile and benevolent beliefs about men. *Psychology of Women Quarterly, 23*, 519–536.

83. Glick, P., & Fiske, S. (2001, February). An ambivalent alliance: Hostile and benevolent sexism as complementary justifications for gender inequality. *American Psychologist, 56*(2), 109–118.

84. Becker, J. C., & Swim, J. K. (2012). Reducing endorsement of benevolent and modern sexist beliefs: Differential effects of addressing harm versus pervasiveness of benevolent sexism. *Social Psychology, 43*(3), 127–137. doi:10.1027/1864-9335/a000091

85. Shnabel, N., Bar-Anan, Y., Kende, A., Bareket, O., & Lazar, Y. (2016). Help to perpetuate traditional gender roles: Benevolent sexism increases engagement in dependency-oriented cross-gender helping. *Journal of Personality and Social Psychology, 110*(1), 55–75. Retrieved from http://dx.doi.org/10.1037/pspi0000037

86. Hammond, M. D., Overall, N. C., & Cross, E. J. (2016). Internalizing sexism within close relationships: Perceptions of intimate partners' benevolent sexism promote women's endorsement of benevolent sexism. *Journal of Personality and Social Psychology, 110*(2), 214–238. Retrieved from http://dx.doi.org/10.1037/pspi0000043

87. Miller, R. (2011). *Intimate relationships* (6th ed.). New York, NY: McGraw-Hill Education.

ACKNOWLEDGMENTS

When I told people I was writing a book about the social pressures women face, the response was always that of great interest. I want to acknowledge that other people's interest in what I was writing about gave me the inspiration, energy, and discipline to continue and reaffirmed to me the importance of this topic.

My colleague **John H. O'Riordan** was the first person to tell me I should write this book. After I gave a presentation at the Royal University of Phnom Penh, Cambodia, he said, "You have to write for the general public, not just academic audiences, because you'll be able to help a lot of women." Thank you, John, for your feedback, which marked the first step on this voyage.

Dorothy Thurman was a great support to me in the early stages of my writing journey. We had beautiful conversations about women's issues. Dorothy was an incredible help when I was writing my proposal; she supported and enriched my ideas and objectives.

I spoke with women from Africa, South America, Asia, Europe, and of course the United States. Some were colleagues; others were friends, or friends of friends. Many of these discussions happened during casual encounters in airports, hotels, museums, parks, gyms, and while networking. I am grateful to each of these women for sharing their stories and inspiring me to persevere and trust my instincts.

Throughout this journey, I had the company and support of many friends: **Lilita Garcia Olano, Linda Duarte, Evelyn and Hernan Contreras, Debbie Rice, Carol Locke, Yolanda Lorge, Debbie O' Neal,**

Mary Peterson, Wasim Hajjiri, Linda Sala, and many more. Thank you for believing in me and supporting me.

My friend **Susana Rigato** gave me personal support, help, and connections. She is to the point and easy to talk with, and I enjoyed communicating with her on a daily basis as I wrote this book. I love her extensive and complex world, where relationships with different people spanning many countries and stages of life coexist at parallel levels. She encouraged this project and had kindly walked with me on this unique journey.

My daughter **Pilar Karlen** inspires me daily. She gave me ideas and suggestions based on her experience of working as an engineer, a typically male-dominated field. She provided invaluable suggestions regarding the format of this book and engaging with readers. We have had so many journeys together and belong to so many worlds! I appreciate how hard she works to be outstanding in her personal and professional endeavors and in contributing to those around her. Pilar's vision and support were as fundamental to this project as she is to my life. I could not have written this book without her.

I also enriched my perspective by talking with men. In my experience, some men are incredibly aware of the oppression and struggles women face and bring objectivity to the conversation. I have spoken and interacted with men like this my whole life.

My dear husband of 23 years, **Greg West,** has appreciated my writing, given me his total focus when I asked for his opinion, been realistic in sharing his views, and supported me through the most challenging times of my life. He is a real and loving partner: my best friend every day, an advisor in my professional endeavors, and someone who makes me laugh!

My father was the man who provided the foundation for who I am. I was the only girl in a family of four children, and my father made me feel important and that I had the same possibilities as my brothers or even greater ones. My father came from a background with very traditional views of women, and I am convinced that we grew together into a new, more balanced perspective. He helped me accomplish my professional objectives, which made me understand and value the importance of guidance in life. I am thankful for his wisdom, can-do attitude, courage, and generosity.

My friend **Walt Locke** enlightened me with his emotional support and humor, and gave me important suggestions for which I am very thankful.

I want to give special mention to my five doctors, who were at my side during the worst moments of my life in the year 2000 when I suffered a severe health problem. They gave me the opportunity for a second chance at life. Thank you, **Dr. Wolfe Gerecht, Dr. Rick Nishimura, Dr. Joseph Dearani, Dr. Malcolm Bell, and Dr. William Freeman**.

Bethany Kelly and her team at Publishing Partner have been excellent, conducting my project from my manuscript to your hands, and always making difficult things easy.

I am grateful to everyone who has inspired, encouraged, and helped me to finish this book, which, in some sense, represents my present mission.

APPENDIX
INTERVIEW SUBJECTS

This Appendix is about essential interviews I had with **Olga Madrigal, Chris T., Lolis Villalpando,** and **Nita Fitzgerald.** These conversations clarified critical aspects regarding the different realities and problems that women in various contexts experience. They shared their wise and courageous thoughts, beliefs, life stories, and learning experiences. *Thanks to each of you for taking me into your confidence and enlightening me.*

Olga Madrigal and I discussed extensively the limitations and pressures women in conservative communities experience, specifically minority ethnic groups here in the United States. The undeniable influence of the patriarchal ideology that gives predominance to men and places women as secondary and submissive, pressured to be "good women," occurs in all settings and circumstances. How women feel overextended with all that is expected of them and then ashamed, feeling they are not good enough. At the same time, if something goes wrong, often women bear the brunt of the blame—for example, if a married man seeks out other women, it is because his partner is not attractive enough. Olga shared how these factors affect women's self-esteem and the associated negative consequences, including how men misuse power dynamics in relationships. I appreciated Olga's sage observation that she looks for progress in her life and returns to the past only to remember what she learned from it, not to stay there.

Chris T. shared her thoughts on the connection between women's internal and external worlds along with her unique perspective on being exposed to two divergent cultures and her objective view of both of them. We talked about her unique journey to follow the call of her inner life, something deeply personal and genuine. We discussed the importance of choice and all its repercussions. For Chris, having her daughter was an immense, significant opportunity to learn the importance of being human. The influence of social class in her family and the rules and standards imposed as part of her upbringing were enlightening. Even if we do not act on everything our parents say, family identity weighs on us and can be liberating or repressive when it comes to personal choice. Another crucial component of our discussions was how our upbringing could leave us vulnerable. Life is about decisions, including choosing options that give meaning to your life. "Whatever it is that gives you meaning, that's what makes you feel good about your life," Chris said. She believes that being beautiful to yourself is what is most important because it affects your heart's deepest feelings about who you are and whom you aspire to be. "We are whom we want to create, and we are all works in progress," she told me. Reflecting on the body obsession that currently affects so many women, Chris talked about the essential responsibility we each have toward our body and health. We are a miracle, and we are in charge of keeping it going, so we have to take responsibility in healthy ways.

Lolis Villalpando and I talked about the ways women react to pressures or problems, such as submission, evasion, or omission, when responding from a place of limited power. Lolis observed that every woman has scars that changed her, which came from moments when she got tired of being ignored, manipulated, or blamed for anything that went wrong. We have to struggle for our life, growth, and happiness and defend these parts of ourselves from social pressures. Lolis described ways to develop personal appreciation for who we are, as a foundation for life and relationships with others. She says there are many shades and colors in life, both light and dark, so we should commit to being content. We can build happiness as an attitude in life. The first step is recognizing that you as an individual are a valuable human being. The second step is to stop complying with others' expectations and make room for your own goals. When you do that, you start to change and become your authentic self, reclaiming the most valuable thing you have: your person. If you can do this, you will do better in interpersonal relationships, especially with loved ones. Lolis also believes firmly in the importance of educating mothers so they can be better role models for their daughters.

My last interview was with **Nita Fitzgerald,** who enlightened me regarding the problematic pressures of sexism and heterosexism and how hard it is growing up when you are different. How much a person can suffer for something that is natural for us: whom we are attracted to. There's no external support because you are not following the expectations of others, and you might not know how to help yourself because you are young and unsure whether your feelings and decisions are right. Nita's evolution toward how she wanted to live her life is a strong example of developing self-respect and open-mindedness. "If somebody has preconceived notions of what my life should look like, that's their problem, not mine." She recognizes her family's positive influence, in that they did not keep her from being herself. She is thankful for that because, as she says, a family is the most important thing when you are young—the prospect of losing them is very scary. She describes her life as difficult but authentic, with many struggles to have others respect her on her terms.

ABOUT THE AUTHOR

Alicia Lamberghini-West, Psy.D. is a licensed psychologist in the states of Missouri and Texas. From 2001 to 2012, she was a graduate school professor of professional psychology. She has had 25 years in private practice as a clinical psychologist, and also extensive experience in psychiatric rehabilitation.

Dr. Lamberghini-West is impassioned by the limitations women face across all cultures, ages, and social classes. She is determined to empower women in every aspect of their lives and help them develop a positive identity in the face of social pressures and challenging gender issues. In 2015, she was incorporated into the Fulbright Specialist Roster for this field.